Christie
Schroeder, LAPC

How to
REALLY WIN
OR LOSE A GUY
in Ten Days

To Dan + Jess —
  May you never follow anything in this book because y'all are too wonderful. Feel free to find me a boy to lose... or win ☺ ... in Nashville.
  I can't wait for you to be in the South with me!!!
    Love y'all to pieces!
         xo
         Christi Schaurly

Copyright © 2013 Coventry House Publishing

All rights reserved.

ISBN: 0615800874
ISBN-13: 978-0615800875

*To my Mom.
The only reason I'm as strong as I am,
is because of your love.*

Contents

Introduction ix

Part 1: The Honeymoon Phase 1
1. This Stinks 3
2. How It All Began 5
3. My Match.com Experiment 9
4. You B. 27
5. Anxious Abe 37
6. The Bar Scene 41

Part 2: Atlanta Meets Hollywood 61
7. My Silver Lining 63
8. Meet Matthew 65
9. Date One: Mishap with a Bra 69
10. Date Two: Wedding Date Stand-Up 73
11. Date Three: I Swear I'm Not Lying 77
12. Date Four: The Lunch Date Re-Run 79
13. Date Five: The Meeting of the Friends 81
14. Date Six: Midnight in the Garden 83
15. Date Seven: Just Friends 85
16. Date Eight: Coast 89
17. Date Nine: Smash 91
18. Date Ten: Concrete Jungle 93

Part 3: Lessons Learned 99
19. Online Etiquette 101
20. Lessons From Strangers 111
21. Lessons From My Friends 121
22. Lessons From My Family 133
23. Lessons From Matthew 137

Acknowledgements 141

Preface

I am not a writer.

In fact, I was a doctoral student in Psychology until I dropped out because I didn't want to compose a dissertation. With that said, what you are about to read is essentially my funny dating diary which took place over the course of several months. The chapters are short and sweet, and you can think of this book as your *dating devotional* to make you feel better about your love life.

The book is divided into three parts: *The Honeymoon Phase*, *Atlanta Meets Hollywood*, and *Lessons Learned*. The first part is devoted to my sometimes funny, often terrible dating experiences. The second part is written about *my* Matthew McConaughey (I'll get to that), and the third part includes my takeaways as they relate to life and love.

If you learn nothing else from this book—and for that, I don't blame you—please walk away with the knowledge that you are not alone.

Dating can be such a joke.

Introduction

I'm sitting beside the Chattahoochee River right now and the stream is flowing. Despite the name sounding like the Moulin Rouge of rivers (i.e., "*hoochee*"), it's quite a beautiful setting. Ducks are at play and richly green woods line the water's surface. In the middle of the river, there are some rocks. The kind with smooth, rounded edges from years of erosion. Just beyond the rocks there's a clearing of still water. Nothing but the water is there. No ducks. No broken limbs. No rocks. For me, this book was written during the rough waters… And I was tired of them.

Part 1:
The Honeymoon Phase

1
This Stinks

To be more exact, *writing* stinks. I hate having to start something new. Have you ever noticed that the beginning of most books can seem a bit subpar? You haven't gotten to the heart of the story yet, and the author is busy trying to paint an elaborate picture so you feel like you're there. All in the hopes that you'll be convinced to read more. It's exhausting to think about. Trying to sum myself up in a single chapter so you'll want to see what comes next seems more than a little difficult, too.

Starting a new relationship feels kind of like writing this book. You pretend to be super cool while getting to know one another. You're not willing to look absolutely foolish or dumb in front of the other person yet. So, you walk on eggshells. Everyone calls the beginning of the relationship the "honeymoon phase." Sure, I guess it is. Only because you haven't gone potty around each other yet. As I heard a little girl put it the other day, "You lie to the other person until he or she wants to go on another date with you." To say that I despise this would be an understatement.

These days, I take on more of a "real approach" when it comes to dating because I can't stand all the superfluous junk. I lay it all out there from the start. I don't love sports. I'm not going to pretend like I do. I'm not a good cook. I never said that I was, and just because I have ovaries doesn't imply that I'm a chef. I'm not a fan of drinking excessively or doing drugs, either. Life is already fun.

These are my non-negotiables.

You'll know these from the start.

There are Rules

I'm a girl. Everything that I'm saying in this book is what I'm already telling all my friends. It's our rule as girls. You boys have rules, too. Don't kid yourselves. You talk about us at the gym and act macho (operative word being *act*), and if we're lucky you'll whisper "I love you" under your breath when you think no one is listening. Both sets of rules are just plain weird. Mine just happen to be in writing.

And so we begin on this stinky ride of the "honeymoon phase" together. There are ups and downs in what you're about to read—often times more downs than anything else. This is why dating is unenjoyable to me, and this is why I wrote this book; to laugh and make it entertaining!

Here's the beginning of how I thought I was going to lose a guy, and what took place instead. This is my real-life version of *How to Lose a Guy in 10 Days*.

2
How It All Began

You're probably asking yourself, "Why would someone willingly choose to start a real-life version of *How to Lose a Guy* when that person will likely lose people and create frenemies?" I wish there was a better answer than what I'm about to tell you, but...I was bored. Of course I wanted to be in a happy relationship and "win" a guy, hence the title of the book, but my dating life took a few weird turns and I felt the urge to write about those terrible dates, too.

We *all* have our horror stories, either on the receiving end of dating, or the giving end. For me, it was mostly the former. I had been on date after date with guys who lost me far before the ten-day mark. I wish they knew why, but I was too passive and not direct enough about the reasons. Likewise, I know that I've made my fair share of dating mistakes, too.

So, I figured, why not do a little dating research to find out what works and what doesn't? Besides, I'm a bit of a research guru myself, having completed my Masters in Professional Counseling and being a newly licensed psychotherapist. I thought I'd devote my dating experiences to this book for the purposes of gaining dating insight, and most of all...to laugh!

As you'll see, I try all the best tricks of the trade to "win" them and "lose" them, and, as it turns out, life isn't as predictable as we may think. You might just surprise yourself by who you like, who falls for you, and how it all works out in the end.

As for me, I much prefer it that way.

How Rude

Hi, my name is Christie. I should probably introduce myself. I've been living in the South for the past seven years, but I originally grew up in the Midwest (go Bucks!). I'm a psychotherapist and I work with every kind of individual, family, and couple that you can imagine. From kiddos to adults, I love 'em all! I live in Buckhead, which is basically the "young professionals" part of Atlanta, although I went to grad school in Savannah. I tend to go out with my girlfriends *a lot*, which isn't always what I'd prefer to do. But when you're young and single, that's just how it is. I pretend to work out, but really can only run a few miles and then I'm done. (I was a cheerleader growing up.) I love to be outside and I try to find as many excuses to be outdoors as possible. I'm a food junkie. And by that, I don't mean that I delight in delicacies and use words like *crudité* to mean veggies and dip. I mean, I eat all the time. I'm hungry even after I finish a meal. In fact, I'm hungry right now. So, I'm always dining out. I like to play tennis and golf, but only when it's done my way. (It's no fun keeping the ball in bounds.)

Patch and I

You'll be reading a lot about psychology in this book. Mostly because it's what I love, but also because it relates so much to dating. So, let me start your psychology lesson off right... *Patch Adams* is one of the greatest movies of all time. The beginning is what helped to jumpstart my love for the profession.

In the opening few scenes, Robin Williams appears to have symptoms of Major Depressive Disorder and, as a result, he admits himself into a psychiatric hospital for help. He ends up being bunked with a person who displays schizophrenic characteristics. This individual ends up refusing to use the bathroom in the middle of the night, and rocks back and forth to prevent himself from peeing his pants because he has visual and auditory hallucinations. He fears that squirrels will attack him from the ground. The profound moment for me was when Patch actually helped this poor guy go to the bathroom. Yes, Robin Williams' character got the man to relieve himself in the actual lavatory. Patch brought himself down to the man's level, saw an opportunity to demonstrate love and compassion, and "killed" the squirrels with imaginary bazookas. He wasn't concerned with how he looked or what other people thought of him. Instead, he did what was necessary to provide help to someone in need. After seeing this, I knew this would be my life's work.

I took my love for helping others and volunteered for a non-profit outreach organization that mentored junior high and high school youths. The premise of the organization was to *earn the right to be heard* with kids so that the volunteers could become positive influences in their lives. In order to do this, we had to meet the kids where they were and develop relationships from that starting point. Rather than asking them to come to us, we had to go to the students. As a volunteer, I spent countless hours in high school cafeterias where I didn't always feel welcome. Time was devoted to coaching dance teams and cheerleading squads, all because we knew this concept worked. People respond to and feel loved by humility.

So, I've decided that's what I'm going to do in my dating life, too. I'm going to meet people where they are (e.g., on dating sites), just like Patch did, and just like I was accustomed to doing in my non-profit work. Rather than asking the guys to come to me at a bar, I'll meet them halfway. I'll be goofy when I feel like being goofy, regardless of what others might think about me. And I'll talk about things I'm passionate about even if it risks "losing" someone. In other words, I plan to be…just me. So, hold on tight. I hope you laugh and smile *a lot*!

> *Disclaimer: Much of what you're about to read may sound shallow, but, as my Uncle Ray once told me, a guy should bring me some depth and then I won't have to be that way. So please enjoy my Seinfeld-esque rant on dating with a fun ending to leave you with hope!*

3
My Match.com Experiment

One more thing about me you should know. Something I forgot to mention... I joined Match.com. I figured that I could screen and meet guys this way, hoping to find some *outside the perimeter* (referred to as OTP in ATL) so that I didn't single-handedly freak out every single guy inside the city-limits of Buckhead. (You know, in case I did anything to "lose" them.) My username is "toocoolforthebar" and my tagline is "I would date the hell out of me." (Please refer to one of the greatest TV shows, *The Office*, for that one.) They both generated a lot of confusion from the guys. Clearly, I'm not as funny to others as I think I am.

After a few days being on the site, I actually gave a Match.com guy my number.

We messaged a few times back and forth, and then he asked for it. I guess that's how it's done?

He also asked for my last name.

Most people have their first or last name as a part of their username. I guess "toocoolforthebar" doesn't give away any pertinent information except for the fact that I'm sarcastic.

Nevertheless, Pimp Daddy (I like to use pseudonyms) and I texted a few times while I was watching basketball with my friends.

The conversation went a little something like this:
Pimp Daddy: Nonsense.
Me: Nonsense.
Pimp Daddy: Nonsense.
Me: Nonsense.

And then this happened...

Pimp Daddy: *"6 months or so. I had gotten the whole bar-hopping, going out 3-4 nights a week with my boys thing out of my system as she and I started to date. Now I like to go out, but in a more relaxed, chill fashion."*

Dead silence.

Pimp Daddy: *"Sorry!! That was supposed to go to my buddy, Kerry. You both texted me at the same time. Kerry is a guy."*

Oh no you di'int.

Me: *"What time is your Match.com date? ;)"*
Pimp Daddy: *"Smart A."*

Umm, watch yo' mouth!

Me: *"I call them as I see them."* (Thanks to my girlfriend, Mary, who knows exactly what to say at all times.)

Pimp Daddy continues... *"You're the one that probably has so many Match boys in her phone, she can't keep them all straight."*

Projection.

Annnd, false.

So, here's a little helpful advice:
1. Keep the ladies straight.
2. Don't project.
3. Own it (i.e., your stupidity) and make a joke.

This is the preferred reaction:
Pimp Daddy: *"Haha, my bad. Guess I got caught."*

Because ya know what, Match.com is a *dating* site! It's expected that you're talking to other girls!

And so he goes down in history as the best Match P-I-M-P.

Christie: 0
Match.com: 1

Eager Beaver

I met another guy on Match.com shortly after Pimp Daddy and I parted ways.

We broke up before we even started dating.

We went for coffee for 45 minutes. He was cute, seemingly funny and witty, smart, athletic (played football in college), the "works." He friended me on Facebook about an hour after we met—eager beaver.

Before I could even wake up the next morning, he texted me: *"I was just thinking... That was some really great interaction/convo yesterday. That's not always easy to find."*

Okay, I get it. A great "interaction" is not easy to find; however, there are several mistakes in the above-mentioned "convo" that sort of make my skin crawl. (Note: I may be a little harsh about this initial text because of what happens later.)

First, he texted me a little too early. Being eager is great if we've been dating for a little while. But now he's gone and friended me on Facebook—he should have just Googled me for now—*and* he texted me before my alarm had even gone off! Secondly, during our conversation at Starbucks, he said that he was so happy that we could talk so deeply about things. (Remember: I'm a therapist. It's my nature to talk.) He explained that he has "the patience of a 2-year-old," so talking deeply so quickly alleviated any of his angst that typically accompanies getting to know somebody for the first time. There's yet another no-no. He referred to himself as an infant.

After I texted him back, *"Yes, it was nice meeting you, too,"* I indicated that I had a long day ahead of me and had to drive from Atlanta to Savannah for school. (Note: This guy lives about 30 minutes south of Atlanta heading toward Savannah.)

And then later on in the day, this happened...

Text from The Beav: *"Driving right past my exit and didn't even say hello... Now that's not the girl I met yesterday."*
Me: *"I didn't know that I was supposed to call on my way down?"*
The Beav: *"Wow. You weren't 'supposed to.' I was half kidding but your response definitely wasn't a nice one. Guess I just got confused with how chatty you were the first day. I'll leave it be."*

He proceeded to unfriend me on Facebook.

Alright, *now* I appreciate that he forewarned me about his impatience; however, his hot-headedness is another thing.

I was being serious: I didn't know that I was supposed to call. I also didn't know that he knew me all that well to say, "Now that's not the girl I met the other day." I wasn't trying to be mean. (I'm sorry you're having a bad day, sir?)

Likewise, he shouldn't have gotten confused with how chatty I was. We were on a pseudo-date! I guess I could have sat there and stared at him, but his patience of a toddler would have probably flared up and we don't know what would have happened then. Further, he should leave the business of formally unfriending up to the girl.

Guess we're not FBO anymore.

Christie: 0
Match.com: 2

Chive On

Martha Stewart has reportedly joined Match.com. If she can be successful at baking cakes and securities fraud, surely she can be good at finding a great date, too. So, even though my first two experiences were less than perfect, I followed Martha's lead and found another guy on the site.

When he asked for my number, I wasn't even slightly hesitant to give it to him because he seemed super silly and fun. So, we started texting and he eventually asked if he could take me on a date. I indicated that I could only do something on Sunday because I already had plans for the rest of the weekend, and, honestly, I didn't want it to be a "real" date.

The night before our date, though, while I was out with some friends and we were texting, I decided to tell him where we were in case he and his friends wanted to meet up. It's better just to skip the weird Sabbath date full of side-hugs and giggles anyways. To my surprise, my Match.com date and his friends actually showed up at Stage Coach (a bar in Atlanta) to meet us. After he bought me a drink and we talked for several minutes, I turned around for a few moments to say 'hi' to a friend, and when I turned back around he was no longer there. He was Houdini and I didn't even know it. Apparently, he felt like he was "cramping" me because I was talking to other people, so, he thought he'd just leave without speaking a word about it. After a little while, though, he decided to return to the bar to try to woo me through buying me drinks and trying to dance with me. And he received a less than warm shoulder from my friends and I.

Annoyed, I stepped outside for close to 20 minutes without him to speak to my friend, Mary, to which he texted me, *"You ok?"*

This is what our entire text conversation looked like... I can't make this stuff up:

Me: *"Did you just leave me?"*
Haterade: *"Sorry, I didn't want to cramp you anymore."*
Me: *"What are you talking about?"*
Haterade: *"Sipping that Haterade, girl."*
Me: *"I have no idea what that means."*
Haterade: *"Me either, but it happened. Lol."*

Fast forward to much later... about 2:30 a.m.

Haterade: *"You ok?"*
Me: *"Yes, Mary and I decided to go outside for a bit. You decided to leave."*
Haterade: *"Bullshit! I waited on you for 20 minutes and you decided to talk to Homeboy* (that's apparently what Haterade was calling a non-fleeing gentleman that I met that evening). *F*ck that shit. I will just eat my pizza and chive on."*
Me: *"I have absolutely no idea what that means."*

Haterade: *"This is ridiculous. I don't even know you. I shouldn't care what you do and vice versa. But, I only came to Stage Coach to see you. Hell, I ran through dumpsters to escape some rando to see you. Then, against my better judge*(-ment, I believe), *I let my friends leave to wait on you and you have something else going on. I mean, come on, man!!!"*
Me: *"That makes no sense."*

At least he has plenty of suitors in the future for himself. Heck, they even chase him down the street, going through dumpsters when he goes against his better "judge."

And that's how I lost my third Match.com guy.

Christie: 0
Match.com: 3

MY 24-YEAR-OLD BOYFRIEND

Not too long after my "Chive On" experience, I got myself a 24-year-old boyfriend. (Not really, but I like to call him that.) I like to make fun of the fact that I met someone so young and yet we continued to talk despite the odds being against us. (I'm 29.) Oh yeah, we also happen to live roughly six hours apart. He's honestly one of the best guys I've ever met. I don't even know where he came from—I literally think he fell from the sky.

So, this southern gentleman and I met the classy way: at a bar. He was the tall, dark, and handsome "Homeboy" that Haterade was referring to in his "Chive On" text. While we were at Stage Coach, we exchanged numbers and became Facebook friends. (Super formal, I know.)

It was on Facebook that I learned he played football in college and read to children through some sort of athletic volunteer program. He also went on a medical mission trip to Haiti where he served as a medical volunteer. Oh, and on an ordinary day in the Spring (i.e., not on Mother's Day), he posted a picture of his mom with a caption that read, "I pray that my future wife will be half as wonderful and loving as my mom." Could he be more perfect?

On top of all that, he was almost like a savior to me after my disaster dates with other guys. He seemed to swoop in after each terrible escapade to restore my faith in men. I wouldn't even have to say anything to him about a bad run-in with a guy, and he was already sending me funny texts or pictures just to make my day. He was my little (well actually, very tall) God-send. And after each awful experience, he made me feel so thankful to be a cougar.

One day I got home to find a letter in the mail. It was from my 24-year-old boyfriend. He had written me a note on a hand-made card from Haiti, and he enclosed a large check for the counseling agency that I work for because we were trying to raise money for a free camp that we offer to kiddos. Inside the card read:

Christie,

It was a pleasure to have the opportunity to meet you! I am glad I built my confidence up in the mirror with my dance moves that night. (When I met him, I teased him about his dance moves. I have a real way with guys apparently.) *But seriously, God puts people in your life for a second or a lifetime, both for a reason, and however long this is for, I can already tell you that you have touched my heart. I wish you the best in your future, and don't forget about our Medieval Times date.* (Oh, because I mentioned it would be fun to go on a

MT date. Seriously.) *Thank you for being you and take care!*

Sincerely,

Your 24-year-old boyfriend

Oh yeah, and I forgot to mention one really small detail. *He used to work at Medieval Times!!* Yep, he and his football buddies worked there for fun a while back. After I mentioned that I wanted to go on a Medieval Times date, he sent me a picture of himself in his uniform (because he doesn't care about what people think) holding a kiddo and wrote, "I found you a Medieval Times date." To say that I adore him would be putting it lightly.

So, I'm not really sure how I "won" his friendship. But, I know how he won mine. He was kind and confident. That's it. And for any of you men who are thinking that girls are attracted to guys who are jerks...you are sorely mistaken. Maybe when we were 20- to 25-years-old, but as we get older and start to think seriously about the kind of person that we want to spend a considerable amount of time with, and who we'd want our kids to be like, it's definitely *not* a jerk.

A friend recently told me that he was concerned about my future with guys because "nice girls (i.e., me) are drawn to jerks," and it just doesn't work out well. Nah. Not true. I'm over them. And I think the rest of us girls are, too. I'd take a Medieval Times working, card sending, children's volunteering stud any day.

I'll end by saying to my 24-year-old boyfriend... Benjamin, you will make some girl *very* happy someday. I am so thankful for you! xoxo

Go ahead and swoon, girls. As you should. Way to be awesome, 24-year-old BF.

Fu Manchu

Now back to my Match.com experiment. Age is a big thing. To guys. To girls. It just is. I'm not about to start dating a 21-year-old at the age of 29. Nor am I willing to date someone in his 50s. It's just not happening. But, I didn't realize how much age mattered to guys until this year. I mean, sure, on the site I had my age parameters (28-35), but they weren't at a *two-year* pickiness level.

I recently almost "lost" a guy by being a little over two years younger than him. I wasn't young *enough*. Apparently it's desirable to have conversations with kids these days. Never mind talking about real world issues...or Seinfeld. She won't know them. Instead, let's talk about Justin Bieber and Miley Cyrus; two kids that I know nothing about except for Bieb's haircut and Miley's twerking.

Yep, this fella indicated that I am on the cusp of being too old for his dating pool. He prefers 23- to 29-year-olds. And I'm pretty sure that I was only thrown into that age mix just to keep my skin from crawling and his lobes from bursting with earfuls of my sassiness. Looks like I'll be out of his parameters in the next year.

A few months ago I received a gem of an email from a fine gent on Match.com, and he wasn't in his thirties. (Have I mentioned how much I love this site?) He was 47-years-old, bald, and had a Fu Manchu.

Fu Manchu writes:

> Hi. I'm too cool for bars, and school, and cloned Starbucks workers who are probably built in a factory with the scruffy beards pasted on. (Met many Match "dates"

at Starbucks.) Well, I'm not too cool for someone a bit younger, like yourself. I'm too cool for people my own age, and marjahn by the pool (oh, that's 30 years from now, but I still won't do it). I do look younger. In the early 30s, except for my especially touched up, too cool, professional photo on my profile that puts 10 years on me. (Clients like older looking.) Why do I want a younger woman: Babies! Ok, and they're a little too cool, too. I'd like to get to know you. And you're funny. How are you?

Memory refresher: My username "toocoolforthebar" was a joke. Repeat. *A joke!* I'm not too cool for the bars. I still go. And clearly I wasn't too cool for anything if I was on Match.com!

So let's review this email. (Keep in mind that I didn't *actually* say the below commentary to Fu Manchu. I only wish I did.)

"Hi. I'm too cool for bars, and school, and cloned Starbucks workers who are probably built in a factory with the scruffy beards pasted on. (Met many Match "dates" at Starbucks.)"

You just opened a can of worms, so here goes... First, please don't play on my idiotic attempt to make light of the fact that I joined Match.com with your overusage of the word, *too*. And too cool for school? When did this become an attractive trait? Second, I love Starbucks. Third, you have no room to be bashing any beards, mister. You lack hair on your head so you grew a ton of it on your face. And what were you quoting with the word, "dates?" Were they not real? I'm so confused.

"Well, I'm not too cool for someone a bit younger, like yourself. I'm too cool for people my own age, and mar-jahn by the pool (oh, that's 30 years from now, but I still won't do it)."

Honey... a bit younger? I'm eighteen years younger than you. Eighteen! And what in the world are you talking about... Marjahn? Is it because of our age difference that I'm not understanding this? The word has a red squiggly line under it when I type it. The word squiggly doesn't even have a red squiggly line under it.

"I do look younger. In the early 30s, except for my especially touched up, too cool, professional photo on my profile that puts 10 years on me. (Clients like older looking.)"

First of all, I have eyes of my own. I can see your picture. I'll be the judge of whether you look like you're in your 30s. Your touched up, professional photo is something we need to talk about. I'm not too young to remember the days of Glamour Shots. There is no reason to have a GS photo on your Match.com profile, whether "clients" like it or not. Are your clients looking for you on Match.com? Further, if that profile picture puts 10 years on you, that would make you 57. Now you're my dad's age. Why are you talking to me?? Wait for it...

"Why do I want a younger woman: Babies!"

Should I offer him my therapeutic services? Never mind being with a woman because you love her. Just take her for her fertile eggs.

"Ok, and they're a little too cool, too. I'd like to get to know you. And you're funny. How are you?"
Good ending. "Oh...and you're funny. Uh...how are you? I just rambled."

Sometimes I wonder how the world operates like this. I can somehow "win" a guy like Fu Manchu, but not a guy who is a little over two years older than me because *I'm* too old...even though I'm younger than he is! It's a wonder so many of my awesome girlfriends are single.

Guess it's time to go freeze my eggs.

Christie: 0
Match.com: 4

Two Weeks' Notice

After these stellar Match.com experiences, I eventually put in my two weeks' notice.

While it can be a great tool for some people, and I totally believe that you can find love this way, I just didn't have the time or patience for it anymore. Before I forget, though, I thought I'd share a few of my other favorite experiences on the site.

First, there's this thing called "winking." You get a lot of winks. It's a cousin of the Facebook "poke." It's a little less-ballsy, but a safer bet than any of the other options.

Then, there's adding someone as a "favorite." This is creepier than a wink, but still less involved than going all out and making direct contact. I guess this means that you become somebody's Queen Bee until they get enough courage to contact you.

Finally, there's emailing. This is pretty self-explanatory, but there's so much to it. I thought I'd break down a few of the best emails I've gotten through Match.com. (Note: I didn't actually say these things to these individuals, though maybe I should have.)

> Anonymous from Alberta, Canada writes, *"Too far for you?"*

Ya know...when I indicated that I only wanted to meet someone within a few miles of Atlanta, I just realized that was a bit idealistic given there are only 6.5 million people in this city. Perhaps I'll go out of state and even out of the country now that you mention it.

> He later writes, *"I still want u."*

I still think you live in Canada.

> Referring to the age parameters that I set on the site (i.e., 28-35), Sugar Daddy, age 41, writes, *"would you consider a sugardaddy? your very sexy woman"*

To answer your question: I lost my wallet and was looking for one. Thank heavens you found me. I am flattered by your assumption.

> Playful Persistence writes, *"Figured I'd flirt again and try a little playful persistence...I'm sure the initial waves of emails and winks must be off the charts. Luv to learn more if you're game. Like your look and what you wrote in the profile. Let me know if there's a nibble of interest."*

Unfortunately, guys, we know how to reach you. If we don't respond, there's a reason. Secondly, "luv," "I'm game," "like my look," and "nibble of interest" all make me feel weird. That's *probably* why I didn't respond.

"You're very attractive and have a great smile. Let me know if you'd like to get together for a drink."
I hit the two criteria to go on a date! Awesome!

In regards to my height preference, Little Guy writes, *"I'm not 6'0," but I have friends that are. Barring that, why don't we grab a coffee or a drink one day?"*
Barring that you just pawned me off on your friends, na-uh.

Casanova writes, *"Come have dinner with me, you'll fall in love ;-)"*
You had me at the comma that you used to separate your two sentences. You really had me at how suave and full of tact you are. And then you reeeally had me at your wink-faced smile.

Young Buck writes, *"Thanks for explaining your username (toocoolforthebar) and tagline (I would date the hell out of me) in your profile because, for a second there, I was confused. Tell me more about you: What do you enjoy doing for fun? Play any sports growing up? Were you a model in a previous life?"*
Bless your heart, but please don't admit that you don't understand my humor (at least not yet). Likewise, I already told you about me in *my profile*, such as the things I like to do and the sports I like to play. I forgot to mention the modeling stuff, though, because *cleeearly* I'm in line with a profession like that.

"You sound like a fun, outgoing woman."
Is calling me a "woman" like saying I look good for my age?

Bearded, grizzly-looking man with black beanie writes, *"So you mayb lik the outdoors, so mayb yr a country girl, yes or no. That are something you like todo on the weeken"*
Honestly, you've got me stumped.

Stone Cold Steve writes, *"Your humor is funny. It's just that some people do not try to make the effort to understand things that are subtle or sarcastic. I have difficulty at times with my humor because it is very dry and sarcastic. My friends and family get it, but most others do not because I do not smile when giving jokes. I feel smiling takes part of the effect out."*
I got the dry part. I guess if the whole not-smiling thing is working for you, too, why fix what works?

"Oh my goodness I just found the future Mrs. (insert name)!"
Oh my goodness...you're joking.

"......TTYS"
Please.

"555-555-5555" (insert real digits)
Really? You've got nothing else?

"Are you a Jungian or a Freudian?"
You've reduced my profession to the only two theorists you know. So, I'll leave you with this..."Time spent with cats is never wasted." - your buddy, Freud. P.S. Psychology-wiz, I can see how many times you've viewed my profile. I'd quit while I'm ahead.

And so I leave you with this... If you're down in the dumps, join Match.com. I promise it'll boost your spirits with the influx of emails, views, and winks you'll receive. But I'll see you offline and out on the town!

(Did I mention that I'm too cool for the bar?)

4

You B.

Following my Match.com failures, I dated a guy for a hot second. His name will go unmentioned, but he's been a buddy of mine for a while. At the end of our pseudo-relationship (I mean, we literally "dated" for a few weeks), he told me that if I was a b*tch, he'd like me more. It's funny...that word has so much power behind it. When I was a little girl, I used to take my dog, Gypsy, outside every day after school to let her go potty. Every now and then, rather than calling her by her real name to beckon her toward me, I'd whisper the "B-word" (she was a female dog) because it made me feel cool and sneaky. (It's weird, though—I would also substitute the word "cuss" for a swear word because I felt too guilty saying an actual cuss word. So, if I stubbed my toe, it would be, "Ah, cuss!") Little did I know the B-word would have such serious implications on my life as an adult.

Let me explain...

I have a friend who dated a guy for almost two years. She did everything for him—cooked, cleaned, visited, befriended his family, came bearing gifts. You name it, she did it without being asked. He, on the other hand, paid no attention to those things and barely lifted a finger for her. But, did she complain? Nope. She was a nice girl.

During this same time, his cousin was dating a girl. This girl was just like my Gypsy. She barked at him, called him names, and told him what to do. She would make him so angry that they would get into screaming matches, ending with objects being thrown across the room. She would even brag about how she'd test her boyfriend to see if he'd do absurd things for her, and he would. She, in turn, would laugh and make fun, emasculating him. They are now engaged and planning to be married.

Couple #1 ended things.

So, it got me thinking about this whole "Gypsy" (i.e., b*tch) thing. Why is it that guys stay with the Gypsies of the world? Guys say that they want their freedom, and if they date a nice girl, they'll get their freedom. The Gypsies, on the other hand, keep guys on a short leash and tell them what to do. So why do guys stay with them? Here's my theory: Guys want Gypsies because they are unpredictable. You never know what a Gypsy is going to do—they often fly off the handle and demand their way. Predictability, on the other hand, leads to certainty, and certainty leads guys to feeling like their freedom has been robbed.

If every day you are certain of what will happen (e.g., you will receive love lavished on you from your girlfriend), it can feel like your freedom has been stripped from you because you know what to expect. Life no longer feels like a choice. But, if you're with a Gypsy, they provide you with an unpredictable box of crayons. If eaten by your special gal (and she may likely eat them; remember, she's unpredictable), you never know what color poop she is going to give you.

So, men wanting Gypsies: Eat cuss. And girls...remember that Gypsies get called the B-word under the nice girl's breath.

My Grocery Store Nightmare

So, back to the guy that told me if I was more of a Gypsy, he'd have a greater affection toward me. We're still friends. Like all the rest of them. So, no harm, no foul. He knows that I'm writing about him, too. (Hi, buddy!) Anyway, the night he told me I was "too nice" of a person for him, he decided to drink a little too much and strand me at the bar for another girl that caught his eye. She seemed to have more of a "backbone," as he put it.

I'm not kidding... I can't make this stuff up.

So, I was deserted.

Imagine being in a city that is foreign to you (he lived nearly two hours away), downtown, in the middle of the night, totally by yourself after being ditched because you aren't *Gypsy* enough. I felt like I was in a Ben Stiller movie. I thought, *this has got to be a joke*. So, in the pouring rain, I called cab company after cab company, trying to find one that would take me back to his house so I could get my car and drive home.

But, this little bugger had to take me to a bar called, "The Grocery Store." It couldn't have had a normal name? No. It had to sound like another type of venue. And better yet, a really generic venue.

Cab Driver: *"What grocery store are you at?"*
Me: *"No, sir. It's a bar called, The Grocery Store."*
Cab Driver: *"Are you at the Piggly Wiggly?"*
Me: *"No, it's a bar called, The Grocery Store."*
Cab Driver: *"Is it next to a Publix?"*

Me: I must be speaking Spanish.

And *that* was my nightmare, as Vince Vaughn would have so adequately said. I left that city and never went back to see the boy. He called and texted, but I never answered. Recently, he tried to contact me again. I had gotten a new phone and didn't recognize the number, so I answered. When he said his name, I wanted to spit on my phone. Instead, I treated him like a Gypsy for a few minutes—as he had requested a few weeks prior—and he finally apologized. Then, of course, I apologized for acting out of character and I went back to being my normal self.

Now, I'm his dating coach.

And so, I leave you with this: Be careful what you wish for. It may not actually be what you want. At least not in the long run.

Karma is a Gypsy

So, my strand-you-at-the-bar-ex-date not only gave me permission to dissect the following email he recently sent to a lovely young lady, but I've already spoken to him about everything I'm about to share with you. (Remember, I'm his new dating coach... this is my job!)

Here goes nothing.

Dear Anonymous,

So, I would love to give you an update on (yada yada) and see how your business plan progress with (yada yada), etc. is coming along, but I'm gonna ask you a series of simple, very related questions instead. The BIG one: Should I still be pursuing you? The follow ups: Did I piss you off (yada yada) weekend, either at your house or at (yada yada)? ((I was feelin' very little pain at (yada yada), so I don't recall our conversation that we had outside...sorry!)) I realize you said to give you "a few weeks," but does that mean don't even contact you un-

til those few weeks have passed? Even with simple, little, random texts or Instagram comments? If so, I've broken those rules on several occasions, and for that I apologize. I'm not a crazy, psycho dude who is gonna be blowing you up all the time. Of that I can assure you. I'm also not a dude in search of a wife. Not there yet in my life. Of THAT I can also assure you. I'm just a good guy who had a great first date with a great girl who is starting to think that maybe said great girl doesn't feel that said good guy is so good anymore. I told you a couple weeks ago that you are worth being patient for. Still feel that way. Just that, in a typical situation, when a guy gets no response to anything, he starts to back off because he realizes that the girl has likely had a change of heart. So, he moves on. But in our situation, the guy has been told "be patient with me" and "it could be a few weeks." Which is cool. But you see, Anonymous, I am used to those aforementioned "typical situations," so my gut tells me to move on. But my logic says don't let this great girl go without at least asking her a series of simple, very related questions as I have just done.

P.S. My gut also tells me that I probably missed a key piece of information in that conversation we had outside of yada yada. Not happy with myself for that one. Still kicking myself for it.

Anyway, sorry to be so wordy. Hope you're doing well. I can see via my Instagram "stalking" that you are ;) I'm great. Other than this conundrum which I've just presented to you!

Later (hopefully)!
Anonymous...a good guy

P.P.S. I'm not expecting you to write an essay, as I ended up doing (wasn't plannin' on that when I started!), in response to my email. Just some kind of a sign that A) I should remain patient, or 2) I should move on. Although if it's B, then a simple explanation would be greatly appreciated so that the same mistakes (if there were any) can be avoided in the future.

Whew! Wow...yes...that just happened.

Let's break this down one at a time, shall we?

"So, I would love to give you an update on (yada yada) and see how your business plan progress with (yada yada), etc. is coming along, but I'm gonna ask you a series of simple, very related questions instead."
No. Don't preface an email with "I was going to do something, but instead I'm doing this," especially when she's likely going to dread whatever she's about to read.

"The BIG one: Should I still be pursuing you?"
You did not use all caps to indicate that she should feel scared. And why in the world did you ask her this question? You either pursue her or you don't—you'll get some sort of a clue. Don't ask! Even *if* she wanted you to "pursue" her, a) that's such an icky way to word it (pursue - really?), and b) she probably won't say, "Gee, yeah, I'd really like for you to PURSUE me."

"The follow ups: Did I piss you off (yada yada) weekend, either at your house or at (yada yada)? ((I was feelin' very little pain at (yada yada), so I don't recall our conversation that we had outside...sorry!))"

Yikes. First, "piss off" is a pretty heavy phrase. Perhaps use "upset you" instead. And it sounds like you're the one that's actually mad at her. But, for what reason? Likewise, you just admitted your belligerence. That's not attractive.

"I realize you said to give you "a few weeks," but does that mean don't even contact you until those few weeks have passed? Even with simple, little, random texts or Instagram comments? If so, I've broken those rules on several occasions, and for that I apologize."

I just don't even know where to begin. If she told you to give her a few weeks, that means she doesn't want to talk to you for a few weeks for whatever reason. She's either busy or not interested. I would err on the side of the latter, because even if she was busy, she'd find time for you if she was interested. And why are you asking her if it's okay for you to text or leave Instagram comments? Isn't that something that you just do, and if they respond, then great? Further, why are you apologizing?? Stop.

"I'm not a crazy, psycho dude who is gonna be blowing you up all the time. Of that I can assure you. I'm also not a dude in search of a wife. Not there yet in my life. Of THAT I can also assure you."

Oh brother..."Psycho dude blowing her up?!" Also, the "dude" in search of a wife business should just be omitted entirely from your vocabulary. While I realize that this is entirely true about you, no girl wants to

hear that...even if she's anti-marriage. It's just weird to throw that out there. It's also a bit presumptuous.

"I'm just a good guy who had a great first date with a great girl who is starting to think that maybe said great girl doesn't feel that said good guy is so good anymore."

Wait, are you talking to her or about her or through her or about someone else? I'm so confused.

"I told you a couple weeks ago that you are worth being patient for. Still feel that way. Just that, in a typical situation, when a guy gets no response to anything, he starts to back off because he realizes that the girl has likely had a change of heart. So, he moves on. But in our situation, the guy has been told "be patient with me" and "it could be a few weeks." Which is cool. But you see, Anonymous, I am used to those aforementioned "typical situations," so my gut tells me to move on. But my logic says don't let this great girl go without at least asking her a series of simple, very related questions as I have just done."

She's just not that into you. Does the girl not take a lunch or bathroom break? Can she not text you before she goes to bed? And please, no more with the third person business.

"P.S. My gut also tells me that I probably missed a key piece of information in that conversation we had outside of yada yada. Not happy with myself for that one. Still kicking myself for it."

Ugh. Stop.

"Anyway, sorry to be so wordy. Hope you're doing well. I can see via my Instagram "stalking" that you are ;) I'm great. Other than this conundrum which I've just presented to you!"

Wait...did that seriously just happen?! Let me re-read. Yep. You just admitted to her that since you haven't been hearing from her, you stalked her, and then told her "I know you're doing well" to basically make her feel bad for not talking to you. Likewise, this "conundrum" is a conundrum for her now. And again, stop apologizing.

"Later (hopefully)!"
Oh gosh, are you a puppy dog?

"Anonymous...a good guy"
Why are you telling her that you're a good guy again? She can figure that out on her own.

"P.P.S. I'm not expecting you to write an essay, as I ended up doing (wasn't plannin' on that when I started!), in response to my email. Just some kind of a sign that A) I should remain patient, or 2) I should move on. Although if it's B, then a simple explanation would be greatly appreciated so that the same mistakes (if there were any) can be avoided in the future."
First, you did a post postscript?? You don't need it here—everything you're saying is stuff you've already said in this very lengthy email. Second, I'm confused, there wasn't a "B" bullet point...just an A and a 2. I get the Chevy Chase reference if that's what you were going for, but it seems odd to throw something so cool in an email as uncool as this. Third, she doesn't owe you an explanation for why she doesn't want to date

you. Why would she? If you're with the right person, you should be able to do all of the "wrong" things.

So, I end on this: Anonymous ex-date friend, karma stinks.

That's all I've got.

And "of THAT" I am not apologizing.

5

Anxious Abe

I went on yet another unusual date following my Grocery Store fiasco. I met the guy while I was out with my girlfriends. He was by himself. It was too late at night for that to serve as a red flag. Woops. It also didn't help that he was really, really cute...and tall! My goodness they grow some giants in the South. And his approach was nothing shy of flattering. He grabbed my arm as I was leaving, turned me around to face him, stared at me for a good five seconds, and threw out superlatives like, "You are the most beautiful girl I've ever seen." My friends can attest to these expedited praises, as they were standing beside me during the whole escapade.

Thanks, discernment... *"Um, sure, you can have my number."*

He called me the next day to invite me to a sports bar to watch the Atlanta Falcons play. How could I resist? He was complimentary (although maybe a little too much), handsome, *and* persistent. I showed up to find the boy sitting at the bar with a ball cap on...yes. I love a good hat (guys, invest). We had our first drink and all of a sudden, Dad walks up. My date had invited his father to meet me. On Date #1. Dad plopped right down beside me and proceeded to compliment my unwashed hair. Like father, like son? While those crazy compliments were *slightly* flattering late at night when

I was practically delirious because I wanted to fall asleep standing up, now it's just sort of creeping me out.

After several awkward courtesy laughs and a few texts to my friends telling them how weird my "date" with Dad was, Anxious Abe asked the bartender to take our picture. He told me that he wanted to show off to his friends how beautiful his date was. At this point Dad also told me how great we looked together as a couple. (Keep in mind, I had known AA for about two and a half hours.) Shortly after this, his friends arrived. (Well, we've got the clan together, is it time to form the band?) Some maintained normal conversations with me while others inquired about how long we had been dating.

I think I had entered the Twilight Zone.

The ending of this story goes a little something like this:

1. AA made several attempts to hang out with me for weeks following Date #1.
2. There were several refusals on my part.
3. I provided AA with countless Come-to-Jesus' (a term we use in the South to indicate a heart-to-heart reality check).
4. I met his friend (details to follow).

Sometimes you just meet a few crazies every now and then. I'd advise you to have a little more insight than I did and to *just say no* when you think something may be a little off. Besides, anyone who approaches you after 2 a.m. with overly flattering statements regarding your beer-stained shirt and smudged mascara is probably not totally with it.

Abe's Friend

Did I mention Anxious Abe had a friend?

Well, here's the story... After my numerous Come-to-Jesus' with AA, he eventually got the hint and stopped pursuing. While I enjoy a good group date with Dad every now and then, that one wasn't for me. A few weeks after my first and final date with AA, one of his friends, whom I had spoken to for quite a while at the sports bar that day (he provided me with a normal, sane conversation), saw AA at a party with another short, blonde girl, like me.

He walked up to AA and his new gal and said, "Hey, that's not Christie?" To which he replied, "Yeah, she wasn't into me." And this guy apparently was more interested in me than in continuing to be AA's friend, because his next question was "Well, can I get her number?"

A few days later, this fella called and we went on a few dates. To this day, he's still a really good friend.

Again, I'm a little perplexed in regards to this dating situation. Why? Because it has become my understanding that similar people hang out together. If you're athletic, you surround yourself with people who like sports. And if you're a little creepy, you're likely to hang out with other creepers. And that's what Abe's friend thought about me. He told me he couldn't figure out why I was on a date with a guy like AA. But, still, we both gave each other a shot, regardless of those assumptions.

So, perhaps every normal group of people has one creepy friend. That's actually not a bad dating tactic...to have one attractive but totally weird friend that can reel in the bait with his looks, and then totally creep her out with his "charm."

Oh, and girls, if you want to go out with a smart and adorable lawyer, let me know. I'll put in a good word!

6
The Bar Scene

Boob-Named Bars

As I write this, I am sitting at an all-male sports bar.

By myself.

Computer and cider on high-top. (Girls, if you're like me and don't like beer, try a cider; it's deceiving to guys because it looks like a brewski.)
I'm ready to go...
I'm trying to figure out why on God's green earth a guy who's looking for a girl would come here. Maybe the majority of you aren't. But I figure there's got to be at least one hopeful young soul expecting to land a number from a gal who either works here or frequents this local all-male hot-spot.
My logic for why this is a bad idea: First, the girls here are *working*. They're not interested in you. If they seem like they are, it's because it's their job. Think you're different? They probably see hundreds of guys in a day. Trust me, we all know you're special, but it's not going to happen.
Second, there are no other girls in this sports bar except for myself. Why? Because us girls feel inadequate when we come here. (The bartenders and servers are half-naked with their twinkies hanging out. Think I compare to these girls? I

think not.) So, now you're at a bar filled with dudes and girls that are *just working*.

My advice? Guys, we know that you want to watch sports. But, if you're looking for a girl, go to a sports bar whose name isn't representative of a female body part, even if the wings *are* great.

And girls, if you're looking for a guy, *please* go to a traditional sports bar. Guys aren't going to be on the dance floor with you and your enormous group of girlfriends screaming along to "Girls Just Wanna Have Fun." It's not gonna happen. Save that for the slumber parties that we have where we prance around in our undies and have pillow fights, because that *really* happens. (Guys, seriously?)

"Oopsies, I Pooted"

I love going out to the bars with my girlfriends. But we always seem to run into some fellas that we aren't too keen on sticking with through the evening.

It happens. Every time. Every place. There's at least one that you're just not too excited about, but he remains a leach with a little liquid confidence in him.

Bless his heart. (Hey, I live in the South, I get to use this phrase, right?)

I recently had one of those encounters, and after forced conversation and awkward lulls, I decided to pull out one of my "lose 'em in ten seconds" tricks. I dropped the bomb (no pun intended, and I promise it wasn't literal)...

"Oopsies, I pooted."

I couldn't believe I had the gumption to say it. Anticipating a disgusted reaction, or at least some unfriendly laughter directed at me, the two guys found it endearing.

Yes, *endearing*.
What??

Apparently, it was "cute."

And it got me thinking... Perhaps it isn't about what we do "right" or "wrong." Maybe you could do all of the "wrong" things, but that certain person will still be enamored with you. I think that's the kind of relationship that we should be searching and hoping for. Perhaps I hung his moon. Let's hope this mooning wasn't taking place while pooting.

That could get ugly.

So, I leave you with my favorite quote from the movie, *Juno*: "Good mood, bad mood, ugly, pretty, handsome, what-have-you. The right person is still going to think the sun shines out of your ass."

Points for me for all of the bum references!

Captain Obvious

After taking a few weeks off from the bar scene so I could catch up on work and life, I finally had a night out.

I forgot how hilarious it can be.

I was at Lost Dog Tavern in Atlanta with three of my close girlfriends celebrating the completion of my horrific counselor licensure exam, as well as my friend, Lauren's, belated birthday. So, she's...ya know...model height with the most beautiful blue eyes and the prettiest, whitest smile. So anyway, we perused the bar as we typically tend to do. We like to find our little nook to just hang out with each other and dance. (It makes sense to go to a bar to just hang out with each other, right?)

On the way to our dugout, I "met" a guy. We were passing one another and he stopped me, gripped my shoulder, and said, "Woa...you're short."

Disclosure: I'm 5'1. I remember thinking when I was in the 4th grade that I was abnormally tall for my class. I felt like the odd man out, as I was having to seriously duck while entering the "Love Tunnel" at school while the rest of the girls could so effortlessly walk right through. (The Love Tunnel is where kiddos would kiss at recess. Mom, I didn't kiss anyone, don't worry.) Little did I know that I'd maintain nearly that exact same height...for the rest of my life.

I responded to this very observant individual with, "Okay." What do you say to something like that? And then the following conversation took place:

Captain Obvious: *"I mean, you're like the shortest person at this bar."*
Me: (long pause) *"Okay?"*
CO: *"Yeah, this probably just wouldn't work out, would it?"*
Me: *"I didn't know that we were working anything out, or that I was up for grabs."*
CO: *"Well, can I get your number?"*
Me: (dumbfounded) *"I'm pretty sure you look like you're kidnapping me right now. I mean, you're like the tallest person at this bar...and, well, I'm the shortest, right?"*

And I proceeded to follow my line-leader through to the outside patio.

So, three things:

1. Master the "okay" as my friend George once told me. There's little to nothing (intelligent) that a person can say in response to it.
2. Girls: If you want to look single, wear heels to the bar. Flats give off the impression that you're in a relationship because you don't care to look good for other guys. (I

was wearing flats, which kept me at my apparently freakishly short height.)
3. Guys: If you're going to be so painfully obvious about something, don't make it about height. Maybe try stating something about her smile—at least you can compliment her that way. I've never heard a guy tell me that he really likes my short legs.

"Okay?"

Pros and Hoes

During my next trip to the bar, something strange happened...I met a former NBA player. A couple girlfriends and I were at a swanky sports bar in Buckhead to watch college basketball. He was there in a full-body track suit. I didn't know who he was. If you know me, this is a typical "Christie moment." The girls were swooning, and I was oblivious. For some unknown reason, he proceeded to strike up a conversation with me. He asked if I was single, to which I replied that I was, and I told him about my dating blog (you're reading the book version of it right now). He asked how he could see it, and if I would text him the link. He then gave me one of his phone numbers (you read that correctly, he had two phones with him), and I texted him the link right then and there.

The following conversation went down at the bar:
Mister Boss Man: *"Do you like to have fun?"*
Oblivious Me: *"Yeah?"* (Umm...who doesn't like to have fun??)
MBM: *"Can you keep our business between us?"*
OM: *"Umm...yeah?"*

And then it hit me...*ew*. He wanted to have fun with me in bed and asked if I could keep my mouth shut about it. And I just noticed his wedding ring, too!

Disclaimer: If you know me, then you know that I am a glass half-full, "you can find a redeeming quality in anyone" kind of girl. Please don't perceive my naivety as stupidity. Life is just full of too many rainbows and butterflies for this gal, and maybe I should perceive it a little darker. For now, the sunshine is still okay with me.

So, the conversation continued:

Newfound Awareness Me: (loudly) *"Aren't you married?!"*

MBM: (embarrassingly looking around) *"Yeah, but shhh. C'mon. You don't have to say 'aren't you married' like that!"*

NAM: *"But you are! And I'm a good girl! And...umm...you should be a good guy and be faithful!"*

MBM: *"It doesn't mean we can't have fun."*

I walked away.

Later that night, at 2 a.m.—while I was sound asleep—Mister Boss Man sent me a text in response to the link I sent him at the bar saying, "you good." Because he was so stinking paranoid about me keeping "our" business to myself, I'm sure he was close to peeing his pants, wondering if I was going to out him on my very public blog. I've kept his name anonymous, but this is what's up, MBM...

First of all, you wore a track suit to a filet-serving sports bar. I don't care who you are or how famous you might be, "c'mon," as you would say.

Secondly, if you think for a second that a girl whom you just met five minutes prior to asking if she wants to have fun on the DL will keep that information on the DL, think again. You're famous. I'm also a girl. Do you really think that I wouldn't tell anybody? (Thankfully, you met a nice one, and I haven't revealed your name. But good grief, not a smart move.) Likewise, when your business becomes my business...it's *my* business to tell. And on the topic of keeping "us" on the DL, let me just say one thing...*ick*. Girls, if a guy asks you to not be the leading lady in your own life (See: *The Holiday*), and wants to keep your life with him in the private sector, run. Don't skip. Don't take a light stroll. Run like MBM is chasing you. There's absolutely no reason for you to be second in line. It's *your* life. And if you let these guys think this about you, then you've accepted the love you think you deserve (See: *The Perks of Being a Wallflower*).

Third, MBM, why do you have two phones? Is it to keep your girls on one and your wife on the other? Thank God we don't use rolodexes anymore. You'd be in a world of pain carrying that weight. Do you also have a pager?

Beep me.

Moreover, now that I know who you are, and now that I know who your beautiful, sweet wife is and how poorly you treat her (she is well known), I can say that you are in an unfortunate position. Guys think they will find better than what they currently have because the relationship has gotten "normal" and somehow *new* equals *better*. (Refer to the conclusion of the "donut experiment" at the end of the movie, *The Five Year Engagement*.) Your loss and her gain, MBM. She is a rock star.

Finally, when you texted me, "you good," I couldn't help but think that you needed a contraction.

You + are = you're.

Oh yeah...

We're in a fight.

We + are.

Am I Getting Punk'd?

After Mister Boss Man and I parted ways, I was fortunate enough to meet a seemingly great guy at a bar just a few days later. I decided that he would be my long-awaited Medieval Times date. So, why him? I'm not exactly sure, but he seemed like he would be a fun companion for something new like this.

In order for him to have my number, he asked that I text him at the bar, and so I did.

Me: *"This is Christie. You're taking me on a Medieval Times date."*
Guy at Bar (I still don't know his actual name): *"You're damn right I am."*

Two days later...

Me: *"So, I heard you were taking me on a Medieval Times date."*
Guy at Bar: *"I was just about to make sure we're still on for that actually. When are we going?"*
Ok, so you're actually being cool and funny. Points for you, GAB.

Me: *"When are you able to go?"*
GAB: *"Good question. I'll have to look at my schedule. When were you thinking?"*
Me: *"Make sure you don't have any other Medieval Times dates on your schedule. I say sometime next week. Wednesday? I'm out of town this weekend and next."*
So, here's the truth...I'm not going to salvage a weekend day for something that might end poorly. Unless, of course, it's Sunday. Sunday is the loneliest day. But,

I'm not sure I want to be going to MT on my Sabbath either.

GAB: *"Next Wednesday should work."*
Me: *"Awesome. Should we double date this one up?"*
As much as this date sounded awesome, I'm not sure that I'd want to go alone. And, I already had a willing girlfriend to go with me.

GAB: *"You got someone in mind? I'm not sure if I'll be able to recruit a friend to drop $50 on Medieval Times."*
Me: *"I do have someone in mind, but is that seriously how much it is?"*
First, who *wouldn't* spend $50 on MT...it's MT! And second, he must have done his research on this one in order to know the cost. Unless he's been before. And if he has, he's a sneaky little devil. I'd be going into this experience blind. That's not fair.

Me: *"How about this, you have your pick: Medieval Times, Fogo de Chao* (a meat skewer place)*, or SkyZone* (an indoor trampoline park with pools of foam).*"*
GAB: *"Hahaha, I've got to give it to you, you're not short of 'out of the box' ideas. Those all sound interesting."*
Me: *"Thanks...so, it's your choice!"*
GAB: (No response.)

The next day...

GAB: *"So, what do you do for a living?"*
Me: *"I'm a therapist. Worst answer in the world to get a date. What about you?"*

No, it really *is* the worst answer in the world to get a date. When I was a special education teacher, you can imagine the guys' responses. Now, picture yourself willingly entering into a possible dating relationship with me where I'll "psychoanalyze" you. And no...I don't actually do that. That's the most annoying assumption that any therapist will ever hear. That's like asking an electrician if he's thinking about all the wiring in a building when he enters a room while on a date.

GAB: *"I think that's cool actually. What kind of therapist?"*
Good question. There are several types. I'm glad you didn't just assume "speech," like most guys.

Me: *"Psychotherapist."*
GAB: *"So, you prescribe drugs?"*
Me: *"No, that's a medical doctor."*
GAB: *"Haha, don't worry. I'm not going to ask for any. I already have a psychiatrist."*

Am I getting punk'd?! No...seriously. That would be awesome if this turned around on me as I was trying to convince a guy to go to MT with me.

Me: *"Really?"*
GAB: *"Yeah, he's the man. I think he's a Jungian psychiatrist. My mom is also studying psychology at the University of Georgia."*

Ok, I'm not even getting into Jungian psychotherapy. You have Wikipedia. Let me just say, it's closely related to Freudian psychotherapy and it's very interesting. If I'm really getting punk'd, he chose for his "psychia-

trist" to have a good theoretical orientation, that's for sure.

Me: *"So, how does your Jungian psychiatrist help you?"*
GAB: *"Well, I reached out right after a bad breakup a couple of years ago and I basically tell him everything, vent, boast, listen, but mostly think out loud. It's pretty nice. What kind of people do you help?"*
Ok, I am definitely getting punk'd. Nice work and touché! Well, I guess I'll keep this going.

Me: *"Wow. That's awesome. I help just about anybody—kiddos, adults, families, couples. They're all mostly underprivileged."*
GAB: *"That's cool. I mentor an underprivileged kid actually. He's a good guy. Ever heard of (insert amazing organization in Atlanta)?"*
Me: *"Seriously? Of course I have. It's a really, really great place."*
GAB: *"I'm in the (insert amazing title within the amazing organization) program, but I spend most of my time with the kid I mentor. Are you involved at all?"*
Wait...huh?? So, I'm *not* getting punk'd?! He's actually an incredible person, and now I was a horrible, terrible human being.

So, the outcome of this story is: I did not go to MT with this guy. He is too sweet for words. I just needed someone either super goofy and funny, or a total jerk for this kind of date.

Knights of Columbus!

I'm with Child

Sure, I've pretended to be pregnant. One time I wanted to get free food that a maternity store was having at their sidewalk event. I get it. Who does that? But, I was passing by and they had cupcakes out. Pink ones. With sprinkles. When we're talkin' cupcakes, seriously, how could I resist? Judge as you will.

But, here's the thing...I've realized there are a*dditional* reasons why pretending to be pregnant isn't such a bad idea.

#1. People are cool with you eating fried pickles (my favorite food), or eating anything in excess (my favorite pastime). And gaining weight is viewed as healthy (amen).

#2. You can wear blousy/babydoll tops (my favorite are Lilly Pulitzer) and jumpsuits/rompers while letting your belly feel free (I love a good romper).

#3. You can hold that little tum-tum whenever you want (because, let's be real, sometimes it just feels good to stretch after a big meal) and receive lots of smiles and "awws." Who doesn't want love?

#4. If you want to be moody (sure, why not?) or if you have a breakout, you can blame it on the "hormones."

#5. You can bring back your inner-Kindergartner self and cut in front of the line going to the bathroom (and take up as much space as you want getting there).

#6. People hold the door for you and offer to carry heavy items. (If I could pretend to be an old lady, I would.)

#7. You can be forgetful and flighty and it's considered endearing.

#8. Not wearing makeup and not doing your hair is acceptable because you don't have the energy or time.

(Although, bypassing the pregnancy bit by wearing workout clothes without having worked out can also work well—just a tip.)

#9. You're viewed as the almighty Yoda because people feel like they can trust you and you're wise. Remember, you're "motherly."

#10. You can quickly lose a guy that you're not interested in because clearly no one wants to be with the above-mentioned pregnant girl (if she isn't carrying your own genes).

On that final note, I'm reminded of a recent night out to Johnny's Hideaway in Atlanta with a few of my girlfriends. (That was the bar featured in the movie *Hall Pass*.) We were dancing to oldies music and having fun. Then, all of a sudden, out from the woodwork, a gentleman approached me. He was tall with dark hair. I'm not sure about the handsome part. (Don't kid yourself, not every guy that comes up to me is a stud...although I wish I could claim that.) He used a line that I had never heard before... "You look like a present."

Wow. Writing that one out even makes me feel a little uncomfortable. I hardly have words for that kind of statement. But, we'll go with it.

My response...

"I'm actually *with* present."

Yep. I sure did. I convinced a man that I was with child as I stuck out my tummy and held it with both hands while swaying back and forth as if to comfort that little bun.

He asked if I knew whether it was a boy or girl (why he didn't inquire about why I was at a bar late at night while being pregnant is beyond me), and I told him that because my belly is hanging a little low, the doctors think it's a boy. The guy proceeded to advise me on waiting to find out the gender since it's my *first* child.

And...he moved on.

I lost that one.

But it looks like I gained a valuable piece of information for my future hubby and I...looks like we'll be waiting to find out the sex of our child, thanks to the advice of this insightful gentleman.

There are just so many great reasons to pretend to have a little nugget in that empty belly of yours, girls. Even if it's due to immaculate conception, I say, go for it.

Christie: 0
Pregnancy: 1

Peacocking

I've had the crazy privilege of having Jim Schroeder as my father. If you're from Perrysburg, Ohio, or are in my circle of friends, that name means something. Why? Because he beats to his own drum and everyone knows it. In 100 degree, Caribbean weather (yes, he's even traveled on vacation by himself), my dad will wear his fur-lined UGG moccasins, his parachute MC Hammer jammer pants with a Jamaican-inspired cloth belt, and a homemade cutoff shirt. (He began cutting apart all of his t-shirts, sweatshirts, and sweatpants because he didn't like the elastic element they all seemed to have. He wasn't trying to start a trend. He was just being Jim Schroeder.)

Nothing more to say.

Coolest guy I know.

If you've seen the movie, *Meet the Fockers*, you already know my family. No conversation is off limits, even if it's about sex. If you want to talk about something, we'll talk about it. No reason to act stuffy.

I distinctly remember being a young junior high girl and having my dad try to pawn off Dale Carnegie's motivational books on me to get me to stop caring about what others thought. If he didn't care what other people thought, why should I? He liked me and he liked who we were as a family, so what else mattered? And if you take a look at my dad's life, you'll see that he's been pretty successful at being just who he is. He landed the blonde-haired, blue-eyed cheerleader with a heart of gold. (I swear to you, if we could see inside my mom's heart, we could make jewelry out of it.) And he's been married to her for the last 39 years. Best of all, he's managed to win over all of my friends. In fact, I'm pretty sure that most of my guy friends used to come over to my house just to hang out with my dad. People love him because he's not afraid to be who he is. And we're drawn to those who recognize their own worth because it means they see *our* worth.

My dad has never hesitated to build myself and others up. And the reason is because he's happy in his own skin. He doesn't need the attention or self-gratification. As I've gotten older, I've attempted—and hoped—to develop more of a *Jim Schroeder mentality*. I think we all should.

With that sentiment in mind, one of my best guy friends and I went to Columbus, Ohio to surprise my girlfriend at her going-away party. (She moved to London for love. I love love.) In order to sneak up on her, my friend and I wore superhero masks as we entered the bar. We succeeded, and it was a great surprise. We didn't care what others may have thought of us. Instead, we just walked in unashamed. But, the interesting part is that this *Jim Schroeder move* worked to our advantage beyond just surprising our friend. We ended up successfully "peacocking." The entire night, whoever was wearing the mask got attention from the opposite sex without even realizing that would be the effect. And I mean, people flocked. (Especially to my Iron Man companion, Marc.) It was an easy conversation starter and it demonstrated to the bar-goers that whoever was wearing the mask was totally cool with just being him- or herself, even if it meant looking like a fool in public.

So, what I've come to realize is that peacocking can be an effective "win them" strategy, if done tastefully. But, you have to be confident like my poppa, Jimbo, and give no explanation or justification for who you are or what you're doing.

You are who you are.

It's as easy as it comes.

Respect.

Reversing Genders

There comes a time when every girl needs to reverse gender roles for a night out at the bar. Why? Because isn't it better to just behave like a guy than to complain about them? And it's exhilarating to act a little foolish every once in a while.

So, I did it.

I started the evening off with a few girls at sushi. I ate my normal (girly) meal in order to prepare myself for the boyish night I was about to endure. I had a seaweed salad and shrimp tempura roll with avocado, cucumber, and spicy mayonnaise, served with a glass of the sweetest white wine followed by an ice cream sundae. I was wearing a classic "I don't care" outfit, which would be comparable to a guy wearing a baseball cap and an unbuttoned, wrinkly shirt with shorts. I wore jeans, flats, a grey, V-neck t-shirt, and a jean jacket. My girlfriends were in silky dresses. I'd even occasionally put on my oversized, plastic-rimmed, Chanel eyeglasses, as if I was attempting to read a book while at the bar.

While my female counterparts sipped on wine and fruity cocktails at the places we stopped, I drank out of a glass bottle of cider. I tore off the label so that it wasn't apparent that the drink I was having was super sweet...if you recall, it's really the only "beer" that I like. (See: *Boob-Named Bars*)

The night began with men approaching my lady friends. One guy assumed that I had a boyfriend because I didn't seem like I was having fun. I was trying to play it cool. I wasn't dancing and I wasn't in cutesy clothes. I was barely interacting with anyone. Instead, I was drinking my "beer" with my eyes glued to a television with football on. (If I was a real guy, I'd probably remember who was playing and who won, but I'm not a guy, and I don't care.) This initial tactic didn't work well. People looked at me like I was a tomboyish brat.

So, I quickly moved on to my next guy move.

The good ol' pick-up line. But, which one would I use? Would I offer to buy a guy a drink? No, that's weird. Would I ask him to buy me one? No, that's pretentious. So, I had to be the corny guy. The one that we all can't stand. I had to be *that* guy with the one-liner.

And my ammo...

I caressed a guy's shirt sleeve (they like that touching on them thing very much) and I said, "What's this material made of?" To which he replied, "Uh...I don't know." And I quickly interjected, "Boyfriend material?" And it was done.

I had won him.

He laughed, grabbed the small of my back as if to show me that the feelings were reciprocated, glanced at my near-empty "beer," and said, "Let's get you another drink."

I realized that what I had always found to be stupid for a guy to do was what actually drew this guy in. Isn't that funny? A guy actually wanted me to be like him. Are all guys like this? I had to find out.

So, I moved on to my next fella and approached him in a similar manner. But instead, I boldly stated that he looked "hot."

> *Note: Guys, please don't refer to us girls as "hot." Not at this age. We prefer "pretty" or even "beautiful" or "gorgeous"...imagine that. "Hot" is a bit wavering. You can be hot one second and cold another, especially when that makeup comes off.*

Hottie's response: "Ah, shoot...I am," as he wiped an invisible layer of sweat off his forehead from underneath his hat. Oh no, I have to relive the torture of telling a guy that he looks hot by *explaining* to him now that I didn't mean that he looked physically warm.

I awkwardly laughed and turned my head down and away from him while scratching near my earlobe, and I said, "No, I mean...you're a hot *guy*." Oh my gosh, the vulnerability. How do guys do it?! *Why* do guys do it?!

And, I won this one, too. He smiled and asked for my number as he was about to head to a different bar with his friends.

Wow. So, taking the initiative and approaching a guy with a pick-up line actually works? Perhaps it takes some pressure off them. It was so uncomfortable for me, I can imagine *why* they'd want a break from it. But, the seemingly careless outfit and inattention to those around me due to a TV screen were *not* desirable. Noted.

So, I had to see about one last guy tactic before I called it a night. If being solely "interested" in sports on TV wasn't going to enable me to meet guys, I'd have to find another hobby that I could talk about that the men might like. Cheerleading? I could discuss my days as a cheerleader or as a coach for sure. Um, no. I don't want to hear about any football plays that a linebacker might have to tell me. Writing? I could get into full detail about my dating blog and how funny I think it is. Well, we know how that would end. Shopping? Seriously? No. I needed to find something *actually* interesting to a guy.

So, I had to turn to my good friend, Marc, for advice. He's the guy that all the girls want to talk to whenever we're out. He's the cute, former college baseball player that seemingly doesn't care about anything except having a good time and laughing. (By the way, he's got a great laugh, ladies! Insert plug for Marc.) He told me to tell a guy that I am a videogame designer. And right now, I am creating weapons and things (?) for a game called *Twisted Metal 4*. Specifically, I recently designed a bazooka for a pick-up truck. (What??)

So, I tried it...and it worked. I had four guys surrounding me, asking me questions about what kinds of things would be coming out for upcoming games, where I went to school for this kind of job, where I'm from, etc. I was blown away. The very thing that would likely turn us girls away from guys is what was drawing them towards me.

I don't get it. Is this how we're supposed to meet Mr. Right? By doing all of the wrong things? By acting like them? I can't do it if that's the case. I was working up a sweat by pretending to have massive amounts of testosterone. (Ah, the irony.)

Perhaps we need to start accepting one another for our differences. Maybe it's time we try accepting people for who they are instead of attempting to mold them into what we want them to be.

I have retired from my videogame designing days.

Ladies who love video games, come out from your dungeons and enter the real world. You'll find yourself a fella in no time. For the rest of us, maybe we need to be willing to at least *learn* about these things if we expect to have something to talk about with the opposite sex. But, we don't have to pretend to *be* like them. I sure won't.

Now it's your turn to learn about *us*, guys.

Part 2: Atlanta Meets Hollywood

My Calm After the Storm

Every storm has a calm. Most people say that the calm happens beforehand. Well, mine came after the storm. I guess that has to occur, too, right? And, well...it was a beautiful disaster.

Somewhere in the mess of all of my disaster dates, I met somebody. But, I had to see if he could handle what the other guys went through. I figured, if he's Mr. Right, then he can put up with all of the wrong things. So, that's exactly what I did. I spread out my "lose-a-guy" tactics (although sometimes unintentionally), even with a guy that I wanted to "win." If being goofy or playful meant that I was being myself, then he was going to see the real me.

These are my ten dates, stretched out over a few weeks, with my Matthew McConaughey.

Atlanta met Hollywood.

7

My Silver Lining

In psychology, there is a behavioral therapy concept called an *extinction burst*. As you may well know, it takes roughly twenty-one days to make or break a habit—good or bad. An extinction burst is basically the *it's-going-to-get-worse-before-it-gets-better* idea in regards to the twenty-one day rule.

I have had this talk with many parents throughout my career: "If you purposely ignore an unwanted or maladaptive behavior of your child, expect it to appear to backfire at first, thus resulting in an increase in the undesired response. But, trust me, hold on tight and if you can make it through some excruciatingly hard weeks, I promise you that it will get better."

A lot of people give in. We do this even when we are trying to give up something as simple as caffeine. Upon foregoing your once-loved Coca Cola, you may initially feel even more drawn to it than you were before. And often times, instead of resisting the craving, you drink the empty calorie soft drink because it becomes too much for you to handle.

I figure that it's got to be the same way with dating. It gets worse before it gets better. Because all good things are hidden (pearls, diamonds, gold)—right? And each requires work to get to because they are covered up by something protecting it. In other words, as time consuming as it has been for me to sift through all the garbage, I've always known that I would eventually come out with something great.

So, I refused to give in to some guy just because he could stroke my ego and become my Sunday night sushi buddy. I knew that I didn't need to end up with a plethora of unwanted guys just because of impatience on my part. But, how did I know that I would eventually come out with something great? The only answer I've got for you is really just an annoying (but true) paradox: *I believed it because I couldn't see it.*

It's just like the air. I know it's there only because I can feel it fill my lungs. I don't need somebody to tell me that it's real. And I've felt love before. Nobody can tell me that I haven't. Love exists, and just because I may not have it right now doesn't mean that I won't have it ever. So, *that's* how I had hope.

If you look hard enough, everything has a silver lining. Mine is that the guys that I "lost" weren't right for me. So, I decided that I *will* have a "win" story. Simple as that. Besides, "I don't want to stay in the bad place where no one believes in silver linings or love or happy endings," as Matthew Quick so eloquently stated in *Silver Linings Playbook.*

8

Meet Matthew

So, I forgot to mention...

The guy whom I almost "lost" in *Fu Manchu* as a result of being *too old* for him (because I am a little over two years *younger* than him)...that's my boy. The guy I've been seeing. My man friend. Boyfriend. Whatever. Let's just get ridiculous with it: Lover. (I just blushed.)

Let me start from the beginning...

It was a disgustingly hot day, and we're in the South, so that means it's humid. It's the kind of day when you stand in the shade and still get no sort of relief. My hair was starting to get more voluminous with every minute.

#whitegirlproblems #secondhashtag #stilldontgetit

My girlfriend and I were at a Braves baseball game. Well, a tailgate to be exact, thrown by this awesome group of people called, *A Social Mess*. Matthew was wearing a blue, oversized baseball jersey and I remember seeing him from a distance and thinking, *Ugh...what a jerk*. Why, you ask? Because I had remembered seeing him a few months prior (couldn't remember where) and he had paid no attention to me at all. (So, naturally, he's a jerk. Right?) And now he was back, looking cute in his stupid jersey. An hour or so went by and my girlfriend, who was visiting me from Savannah for her birthday, wanted to make friends because she doesn't often get to experience the big city life. So, she asked what I thought of him because that's what girls do...they ask.

My reply: *"Ehh, he's okay."*

And then he ended up inching his way closer to us.

So, of course, this "jerk" and my sweet girlfriend talked for a few minutes. And well...nothing came of it for either of us gals. I briefly said "hello," she didn't ask for his number, and it just...was.

We watched as he would get approached by other girls. Two in particular left both my girlfriend and I thinking to ourselves, *What in the world is going on?!*

One had long, fake black hair serving as a lowlight to the platinum blonde up top, and the other had fingernails at a Guinness Record length. They both had low enough cut shirts to feed their children if they had any. And Matthew spent a considerable amount of time talking with them.

After seeing this, I had figured it out: *I guess I know why he's never approached me...I don't think I'm his type.* And I proceeded on with my night, noticing as he would keep to himself and be polite to other girls who would approach him.

I liked that about him. He didn't seem to care at all about *looking* for anything. He wasn't flirting or searching, or frankly...finding. Instead, when girls came up to him, he was kind, even if they didn't appear to be what I would consider *his type* based on his look. Then they would go on their way because he didn't seem all that interested. (You know you're a good person when you're nice to those who can offer you...well, nothing. Very proud of this boy.)

I guess maybe he wasn't such a jerk after all. He just doesn't go up to girls to hit on them. I like that. *A lot.* It might be my favorite thing about him.

And that was our first meeting.

Yep, that was it. A "hello" and a snub.

He's *my* Matthew McConaughey. He's tall with sandy-blonde hair, a perfect smile with pearly white teeth and great smile lines (that's my favorite thing), green eyes, and big arms (my other favorite thing).

I could stare at him for hours.

Yep!

The Rule of Two

Following the Braves game, Matthew and I exchanged a few messages via Tinder. (If you don't know the social media dating app *Tinder*, you might just be living in the Dating Dark Ages.) He was the one who initially reached out, but he didn't acknowledge our meeting at the Braves game a few days prior. I called him out on the fact that we had just met. He reciprocated the understanding of that event by detailing some memories of me from that day (e.g., what I was drinking, my friend's birthday, etc.), to which I was surprised (in a good way). We threw a few jokes back and forth for witty banter (so typical), and asked each other a few boring questions like, "What do you do?" and "Where are you from?" to which we'd both respond to in a matter of days or hours.

I finally gave him my number and we continued this waiting period via our phones. We're all accustomed to this type of behavior. Why, in the initial stages of getting to know someone, do we wait so long to respond? Are we trying to prove that we are important and cool, or that we are just *that* busy that we can't pay attention to our phone? Doesn't everybody typically check their phone every thirty minutes or so? Most of us sit with it face up on our dinner table!

So, why do we play this game?

To be totally honest, I'd have to admit that I'm guilty of those aforementioned assumptions. Yes, I wanted to look cool and important and present myself as if I'm busy doing something else. But, the question is, am I *really* proving to be that special if I'm (obviously) playing a game? Regardless of the answer (which is probably a big fat "no"), my reasoning for participating in this type of game-like behavior is simple... It wouldn't be attractive to the other person if I immediately responded. I can definitively say that I am *not* attracted to a guy who rapidly responds to my texts. Sure, I'll get annoyed if my *boyfriend* doesn't answer for long hours, but a guy whom I hardly know doesn't need to make me his number one priority just yet.

Since we now have sound rationale for playing this game in the beginning stage of getting to know someone, just how long should you wait to respond to a call or text? My good-rounded number would be two hours. It's not too long to totally tick somebody off and catapult them into another person's direction (to somebody who *will* respond in two), but it's not too short to perturb someone with your eagerness.

There's a fine line between being a slow slug and an eager beaver.

P.S. You can't be very cool or coy on Tinder. It shows people when you were last on the site. Don't get caught!

9
Date One: Mishap with a Bra

Date #1 was about as anti-climactic as they come. In fact, I didn't even really like Matthew after our first date. It wasn't that he had done anything *wrong*. No, it was just the timing. I was happy. And content. Life was good apart from him.

We met for drinks at a restaurant called Holeman and Finch—some swanky place in Buckhead. And I wasn't dressed for the occasion. Hours prior to our date, the power at my house had gone out. There was a big storm in the city, taking out lines in my neighborhood. This left me unshowered...and after I had just gone for a run.

He texted, to which I responded, *"The weather is pretty bad. Would you rather postpone?"* For weeks, I had been putting off this initial date. I think he was a bit fed up with that.

So, he said, *"If you'd like, but I think it'll be okay, unless you melt in the rain."*

Well, I couldn't have that high-maintenance image. No way. So, I went. Sweaty and gross. I wore a silk, aquamarine tank top that required a strapless or "sticky" bra. If you're unaware of what a sticky bra is, it's the kind that doesn't have a back and sticks directly to your skin without leaving any residue. For a gal that isn't the most endowed, this kind of attire works perfectly. (Or so I thought that night.) Perhaps the packaging should have included some instructions about not wearing it on dirty skin. Or maybe it did and I didn't take the time to read. During our interview, I mean, date, it started to fall.

Guess it doesn't latch on so well to salt.

Throughout the two hours that we spent together, I went from an open body discussion to arms crossed and looking agitated. The bra ended up nearly inching itself all the way down to my stomach as it detached itself from my skin. And, as we departed, I gave him a frazzled hug and kept my elbows at my waist to keep it from falling. I'm sure I looked like a character out of the movie *Alien,* if he noticed.

And our conversation...it was a bit like my bra. Unattached. It was the typical conversation that you have on every first date. The review of your five-year plan, the lengthy discussion about what Mom and Dad are like, all of your past residences, and your resume and CV. Sure, he was interesting. He *is* interesting. But, like I said, the timing was off.

I had a situation with a shower, a bra, and a happy disposition. I didn't need the addition of a boyfriend.

Warm Shoulders are Overrated

It's a wonder why Matthew asked me on another date after my bra and shower mishaps.

The day after our first date, I drove two hours south of Atlanta for my best friend, Katie's, bridal shower. While I was on my way to the shower, I called an ex-boyfriend to ask him to accompany me to her wedding (which would take place the following month). We spoke on the phone during my car ride and even discussed potential dance moves.

Matthew was so far from my mind. But, why?

He probably could have stood in a line with every suitable gentleman, along with every ex, and I'd still choose him. So, why wasn't I interested? Maybe because I didn't take our first date seriously.

Or maybe because it *takes* a second date. First dates are for the birds. That's what he thought, too. Apparently, I was a nervous Chatty Cathy who was intimidatingly bold. Second dates, on the other hand, are where you're over the nervousness. You do something more fun than conduct an interview. You spend time laughing instead of pretending to laugh. I don't know why the radio silence took place, but I do know that I left our first date thinking that I'd never speak to him again. And lo and behold, he kept showing up on my phone. Maybe guys shouldn't throw in the towel so easily.

I left Katie's shower that day and opened my purse to find another text message from Matthew. Instead of texting back, I called him on my way home. I told him that I was out of town, two hours away, for a bridal shower. I told him that I would be getting back too late to do anything, but I wanted to get together soon. I'm fairly certain he wasn't buying it. It appeared to be nonsense. But it was true. And he *did* eventually buy it. He asked that we go out the following day—a Sunday. (That's almost as uneventful as a coffee or yogurt date.) And I agreed, somewhat sympathetically.

10

Date Two: Wedding Date Stand-Up

Date #2 was anything but ordinary. I managed to somehow win a date with Matthew after my incessant refusals to be normal. And on this one, I approached him, as I had arrived late. He was sitting down at Park Tavern, a bar/music venue in Piedmont Park. (Great date spot in Atlanta.)

Strike on my part for being tardy.

I almost didn't recognize him as I was walking up. He had sunglasses on and a big bandage plastered to his forehead. He stood up, we hugged, he complimented my black-on-black outfit (I wore a black tank-top tucked into a pair of high-waisted black shorts with an oversized camel-colored belt), and I laughed, saying how unusual it was for me to wear black. That was another thing that I thought would have backfired. I dressed out of character for myself. I'm usually adorned in the typical Southern girl's attire on most summer days. Bright colors paired with even brighter colors, scalloped shorts, seersucker, and stripes. But on this day, I dressed a bit more edgy. I'm a city girl now, why not? And this Southern guy actually liked it.

And, then, I fell.

No, not literally.

Figuratively.

He took off his sunglasses and he was finally a real human being. Before, he was just some hunky-looking guy who I thought probably wanted another girl to add to his roster. He was also just somebody behind a telephone that I didn't have to care about. And to him, I was a Space Cadet, off in La-La Land, chatting away when we were together and ignoring him when he wasn't with me.

But on this day, he had bruises and scars, and a little blood. He had gotten into a late-night wakeboarding accident over the weekend while I was at the bridal shower.

When he took off his sunglasses, I immediately clasped my hands over my mouth to prevent my awe from being displayed. I inquired as to whether he had gotten into a fight. (It would pretty much be over at that point if that was the case.) He laughed while acknowledging that while it definitely looked like it, it was just his wakeboard battling his face after hitting a wake.

Matthew couldn't quite remember the whole story due to his blacking out at the time, but the giant scar seeping out of the bandage was an indication of the event. And the blood in his eyes was so sad. I couldn't believe that I had ignored him. And I couldn't believe that he showed up to our date like that. I almost didn't show to our first because of a lack of a *shower*. But, here he was, unashamed to be seen by me.

I hated falling that day. It wasn't in my plan. I wasn't supposed to like him. I was happy. I was dating around. But, it was on that day that I decided to stand up my original date to Katie's wedding.

Matthew and I discussed both being dates to upcoming nuptials that we had to attend. Mine was my best friend's. His was a family member's, and in two weeks!

Goodbye, ex-boyfriend. Hello, potential new one.

11

Date Three: I Swear I'm Not Lying

After several texts and phone calls, date #3 was another lunch, this time at Houston's. We met there. I don't do the whole ride/pick-up thing just yet. It was at a restaurant he had selected. He was always good about that. Having a plan. Asking if I was okay with it.

Thankfully, my dates with Matthew were always somewhat planned, with a backup plan in place. They were driven by the both of us during the date, making the conversation and experience fresh and new.

And I wasn't taken aback by my third date with Matthew, which happened to be during the day. In fact, I appreciated it. It showed that he wasn't trying to "get" anything from me because it wasn't a 2:00 a.m., cocktail-filled night. And I made my appreciation for that day-date known by reporting that I "take things slow." I don't even know what I meant by that. I think I was trying to say that I don't want to rush anything. I'm not sure if I had a specific pace, but I guess time would tell.

On this date, as much as I was enjoying our reciprocal conversation, I still felt a little funny because I wasn't used to going on consecutive dates with anybody. This made me a little uncomfortable. You see, we appeared to be in a *relationship*. We laughed and had a great rapport. Our friendship started off quick with no lulls in any conversations. It just looked natural, and I noticed that people assumed we were together, too. In fact, a waitress asked if we were dating, and I jokingly replied, "Nope, we're actually *engaged*!" I was frantic. I had to alleviate the awkwardness. I figured he felt strange about the assumption, too, so I didn't want him to think that I was okay with looking like we were a couple. I *had* to make a joke. I was hating life at that moment. (I have a way of digging myself into icky-feeling situations and then trying to find my way out.) Thankfully, my roommate texted me and broke up the awkwardness. She's known about my former terrible escapades with guys, so we had jokingly planned for her to text me an "escape" for a previous date. Maybe she was thinking that I needed an out with this one, too. But this text was real, and it told me she was sick and had to go to the hospital. So, I used the ever-popular, "I swear I'm not lying" phrase. I'm not sure if he bought it, but I rushed out of there, leaving him with the bill. Oh my gosh. What a terrible series of events. I thought to myself, "Have I *finally* lost him?"

12

Date Four: The Lunch Date Re-Run

I don't know how I did it, but apparently Matthew was okay with pretending to be hitched to me in public.

Date #4 came just a day after Date #3, and it was a lunch date. *Again*. Is there something wrong with me? Perhaps this is karma. I get it. If I had a female dog, I'd name her Karma.

Well, my karma-filled date involved a car ride pick-up this time. Big step. (I figured he wasn't going to kill me now if he hadn't already killed me after my wedding proposal at Houston's.) I was wearing a lovely Lilly Pulitzer babydoll top. You know, the kind that bells out at the bottom. My friend, Hogan, once told me that this shirt makes me look like I'm wearing a small child's dress.

Unlike the other dates, on this one, upon seeing me, Matthew didn't say that I looked nice. He said nothing about the way that I was dressed or how I looked.

I figured it was a fail.

But, we went on to lunch at Treehouse in Peachtree Hills. The conversation was normal, and so, of course, I wasn't having it; therefore, I turned it into the annoying "what's your favorite ____" game. You know, the one that you probably played at the YMCA summer camp when you were a kid, where you all sat around in a circle and dished about what makes you "tick," as in your favorite color, pizza topping, and sport. And by golly, we did the same thing that day, and Matthew went right along with it.

For whatever reason, there was no breaking this guy. Not that I was trying to. I was just being myself and if I wanted to do something, I did it. But, it was a bit shocking that he was putting up with my childish ways. I dressed like a kid and acted like a kid on this date. And he stuck around.

Which I was okay with.

For once.

Before this time, I didn't believe in crazy love. I only believed in what was ordinary...what made sense.

13

Date Five: The Meeting of the Friends

Date #5 seemed like the right time to meet the clan, and that's exactly what it was. Finally, it wasn't a day-date. It was a Friday night, and my two girlfriends and I were out having tapas at a place in the Highlands, and Matthew and his friend, Keegan, decided to join us. I was expecting Matthew to have some extremely good-looking but terrible (as in player) friends. I guess that wasn't fair. Just because Matthew is cute hasn't made him scum *yet*. I doubt that he was expecting Barbies as my friends. But, I judged. Sue me.

Instead of a frat boy clone, though, in walked an intelligent and funny guy of a different ethnicity. Someone with a huge smile and a warm hug. I was shocked. He talked to my friends. He didn't drink. He was polite and opened doors. Matthew hangs out with people like this? Don't get me wrong, it's not that I didn't think that Matthew was smart or funny, warm or friendly, polite or chivalrous. I just thought that maybe there was only one of him in this world. And that this someone I landed upon was a fluke of a human being. And to be honest, I was waiting for the bad news. Everything up until this point was pretty perfect. Matthew looked perfect, he acted perfect, and even with his imperfections (e.g., his mangled face and interesting heartbreak stories), he was still perfect. I didn't think that he'd have perfect friends because that would mean that my assumptions were right: He was too perfect. And I didn't need to wait until the bomb dropped on my hope.

What was I to do now? This intimidated me. This would likely cause me to lose him. This made me even more anxious and nervous than I already was at Houston's, the day I told our waitress that we were engaged.

Engaged!

KISS

Is it possible to miss someone you've never met?

Maybe because you know what you're looking for and you realize you don't have it?

That missing feeling, and the hope that I have is "the sun that leads me to the light," as Phillip Phillips so eloquently puts it. And better...it's *the reason I believe in something I don't know*. I don't think that I'd be created to miss something if it didn't exist. Maybe Matthew is the existence of that.

So, maybe I should just Keep It Simple, Stupid.

And stop being intimidated.

14

Date Six: Midnight in the Garden

Date #6 was preceded by a perfect Date #5. On that fifth date, our friends meshed. Everything went so well. When I came home that night, my girlfriend and I talked about how sweet Matthew's friend was. But yet, there was still something missing. The signs were there, but I hadn't been kissed yet. Did he even like me? I was being taken on day-date after day-date, picked up and dropped off, and without so much as a full frontal hug upon our "goodbyes." We had only been giving each other side hugs with pats.

So, that night, I figured I'd get my kiss.

On the day of our sixth date, Matthew sent me a link to the Atlanta Botanical Gardens and asked if I wanted to go. Of course I'd go. It was an evening full of music and cocktails.

I wore a dress with wedges (we are over a foot apart in height, so I needed to make the kiss a little more feasible). Besides, it was a real date and that called for wedges. Matthew picked me up and when we arrived, it was the most picturesque place I could have imagined. We got our drinks and began walking around through beautiful trees and flowers to tunes from a jazzy saxophone player. And just as we had spent nearly twenty minutes there, something quite common to my world happened. It started to downpour. Thank God I didn't decide to wear anything white. A girl's gotta think about that when she's wearing a dress with a built-in bra. (I was over the whole sticky-bra thing.) The downpour led to people fleeing to find shelter and vendors taking cover. But, we embraced it. Matthew and I walked around for a little bit longer...in the rain. In fact, we were probably the last people that ordered any drinks...in the rain. It was exhilarating and fun.

Finally, after a while, after I had been shivering for what seemed like an eternity, we decided to stand under an awning. It was the perfect moment. It was so romantic. The music was no longer playing, but the sound of the raindrops set a perfect harmonic background for a first kiss. But instead, 40-something-year-old Steve had to show up. (One of the bartenders that I was friendly to earlier.) I invited him under our awning because I felt bad for him. Funny how that seems to be a trend with me. The feeling bad for a guy thing, that is. The rest of our night involved conversations with Steve about his church, his hometown in Michigan, and his four children.

Yes, that was it. There was no goodbye kiss at the end of our date. Not even an embrace in the rain. I think my *How to Win a Guy* strategy worked and I had found myself a nice *friend*.

15

Date Seven: Just Friends

Date #7 was unnerving because I just wanted to kiss the boy. It was a day-date on a Friday afternoon at another lunch spot.

Perhaps Matthew is gay, I thought.

But, the signs weren't there. Maybe he's seeing somebody else. Yeah, he's probably seeing somebody else. Well, fine. I guess I better find somebody else, too. My mind raced through every possibility.

On this date, I was quiet, which was out of the ordinary for me. It was a quick meal where he could tell that something was going on inside my head. I was a little annoyed because I couldn't tell him what was on my mind. Because you can't have a DTR this early. But, I wanted him to be *my guy*. The problem is, I'm not one of those people who can hide their emotions easily. I wear my heart on my sleeve. (My mom always says it's my best and my worst quality…it allows me to love and be loved, but it can also hurt me if I'm not careful.) And well, shucks. I didn't have anybody else to go on a date with if he *was* seeing someone else. And even if I did, I don't know if I could go through with it. Once I'm partially invested, I'm fully invested until not invested anymore. Why couldn't he be like that, too? But, this problem wasn't going to distract me from acting curt. And I did just that.

Later that day, Matthew texted me to ask what my plans were for later that evening. I told him that I'd be going out with my friends, to which he proceeded to ask, "Where to?", and I replied, "I'm not sure, but somewhere in Decatur; that's where my friends want to go." I figured I'd have a night apart from the guy since Decatur is OTP and considered a nuisance to travel to when you live within the perimeter. But, Matthew had other plans. He rallied up one of his friends and they met us in Decatur that night. I was shocked. Because, again, I figured he was either gay or a player. I couldn't figure out why I was being strung along without even receiving a full hug from the boy.

But, the evening turned out surprisingly well again. He paid attention to me, even though his friend was there. We had moments where it was just the two of us, laughing and talking. We were dressed for the occasion, he in a neutral outfit with loafers on, and I in the same color scheme with heels.

It was time.

So, I drank some liquid courage before leaving the bar, and in the car ride home, I asked Matthew if he liked me. (Word to the wise: I find it to be a bit unattractive to have a serious talk, tipsy. I'm sure he did, too. Don't do it.)

He seemed shocked. What is there to be shocked about? I made myself clearer: "We keep going on all of these day-dates, but it doesn't seem like you like me." And as he pulled into the parking lot to drop me off, Matthew got out of the car. He walked around to the other side, reached for what seemed like a (real) hug, pulled me up against him, and hand on face, he kissed me.

Finally!

A real kiss. Standing. Embraced.

And it was goood.

Meanwhile, my two girlfriends were pulling up in the other car, honking to make it just *that* much more romantic. As if the parking lot wasn't already enough. And after my girlfriends walked inside, giving us our public parking lot privacy, Matthew said, "Was that what you were referring to? Because if it is, I've been wanting to do that for a long time now, but you said that you wanted to take things slow."

Perfection.

16

Date Eight: Coast

After we got our first kiss out of the way, Date #8 was a breeze. We coasted right through it at a restaurant called, Coast. (Pun intended.)

Upon entering the restaurant, I saw a girlfriend from Savannah who now lives in Atlanta. She's a friend of mine who manages one of my favorite clothing stores. I mentioned to her that I was excited to wear my new pair of heels. You have to unamuse (not a word) a guy every now and then.

As Matthew and I were about to be seated, I told my friend that I was *actually* on a date, and emphatically, I stated that it was with Matthew.

I neglected to inform you of one thing: On Date #1, I told Matthew that I was a dating blogger. Matthew wasn't in the dark about what he was getting himself into. In fact, he later told me that he originally thought I might be a bit caddy since I write a dating blog. Nevertheless, he continued to see me, without ever reading my blog. That was one thing that I loved about Matthew during this time. He wasn't trying to learn my tricks of the trade or what makes me tick. He wanted to get to know me authentically. And well, that strike at making him seem like a piece of blog meat to my friend didn't phase him either.

After leaving Coast, we ended up going to a bar to meet up with one of Matthew's friends. At the end of our night, his friend jokingly said that if things didn't work out with Matthew, I've got a shot with him.

#winning… the friends

17

Date Nine: Smash

Date #9 was a bit more casual. You could see that Matthew and I were becoming more comfortable with one another. I wondered if anything was going to break this. I didn't want it to, but there had to be something, right? Stuff like this doesn't happen in real life, at least not to me.

We went to dinner at a sushi place that caters to my every need. I ordered the most ridiculously detailed roll that wasn't even on the menu. If humans were dogs, I'd be a poodle at this point. He seemed unphased. Why wasn't he thinking that I was high maintenance? Or maybe he was and Matthew was just a good actor. Whatever the reason, he stayed involved and continued to seem interested.

Our conversation was just as on point as always. Except we were moving from the *what-makes-you-you* talk to real-world discussions about our jobs and frustrations. We left the restaurant and Matthew wanted dessert. Across the street was a cupcake store, so we decided to peruse the venue for about ten minutes until choosing our beloved frosted mess.

Things were good and our cupcakes were yummy when all of a sudden Matthew asked to try some of mine. So what did I do? I decided to smash it in his face. What was gonna give?! I had to push his buttons a little. But, instead of being prissy about it, he reciprocated the love. And our cupcakes became our new face décor.

Gosh, I was crazy about him then. We were becoming foolish friends.

"If You Fall, I Fall"

When I was a senior in high school, my best guy friend and I were both on Homecoming Court. His name is George. I call him "GP" for short. (Come on... Georgie Porgie?) He calls me "Swoda." (Imagine being a child with a speech impediment attempting to pronounce my last name *Schroeder*. That's what you get.) He's the best. He's super funny and smart, and a really, really great friend to me.

Anyway, I waited until the last minute, as usual, and didn't get a dress until three days before the dance. In fact, I didn't even *get* a dress; I borrowed one from a friend. As a result, I couldn't alter it since it wasn't mine, and thus, this became a serious (it was high school) problem because it was too long for my short legs. The problem wasn't that it was too long to dance in, though. No, it was a problem because the Court had to walk down a flight of stairs that opened onto a platform surrounded by glass, which overlooked a common area in front of hundreds of people. It was likely that I was going to trip and fall. I could just see it...face planted on the platform. Puppy dog eyes as I look up. Not embarrassing (or painful) at all. So, before they opened the doors for us to enter down the staircase, I was quite nervous and GP could tell. With brotherly affection, he said, "Dude, if you fall, I fall."

Right then and there, he made a pact with me. He was going to keep a peripheral watch on me, and if I fell, he would take the fall, too. I guess we'd say that the floor was slippery? Either way, he was willing to look foolish for his pal. In front of everyone.

We didn't fall.

He was there for me, just like Matthew.

18

Date Ten: Concrete Jungle

Date #10.

So, this is it, right?

This is supposed to be the date by which I was going to lose Matthew if I was ever going to. Nothing seemed to budge with him, though.

We somehow battled through my being "too old" for him. We persevered through a mishap with a bra, his mangled face, my sick roommate, an uncomfortable engagement, my high-maintenance antics, and plenty of day-dates. We went through literal rainstorms, with him being "too slow" and me being too caddy, all within ten dates. And *somehow*, we made it out stronger.

By Date #10, we were off to New York City for a weekend getaway. We stayed in the Hamptons and in the city, and we had an absolute blast. Despite one time when I was frustrated with *his* childlike ways (oh sure, he seemed perfect, but he wasn't, just like the rest of us aren't), everything was great. A relationship was established by the end of our trip. And that's all that matters.

So, then what happened?

Well, I fell in love.

This is Love

My mom is the definition of the word, *lovely*. Everything she exudes, everything she is, she is just...perfect. The way she reminds me of home, speaks my thoughts, and replaces fear with hope. Thinking about her not being in my world almost makes it hard to breathe. Since I was a little girl, she has been my confidant and best friend. The keeper of my secrets. I wish all girls had this kind of relationship with their mom.

I remember a distinct moment from my childhood when I realized just how lovely she was. It was when I was young and a boy from school didn't like me.

Through boxes of tissues and snot running down my face—which she wiped off onto her sleeve—I looked at her and thought to myself, *I know this isn't a big deal to her, but she's acting like it is. Because it is to me.* And that's when I really knew my mom loved me. At that moment, I realized one thing: that her tears resulted from my tears, and I thought, *this is love.*

I had a similar revelation with Matthew a few months after our tenth date. We were out with some friends one night, drinking some cider. For whatever reason, we started discussing a trivial concept with the group. It was a concept that I am usually having to defend all by myself. It was something that I am passionate about, and it typically causes a great debate amongst groups of people. Without ever having discussed the topic with Matthew, and before I ever had to speak up in the group, he had already interjected into the discussion and single-handedly refuted all of our friends' notions as a means to advocate for my cause. He had no way of knowing how I felt about it, but he felt the same way about the matter. I actually got to sit back for once, without having to debate. I watched as the man that I had been rapidly falling for turned my infatuation into real feelings. And again, I thought to myself, *this is love.*

It was in that moment that I realized what Chelsea Handler, one of my favorite girls of all time, meant in the movie, *This Means War,* "Don't choose the better guy. Choose the guy that makes you the better girl." Not only was Matthew the right option for me—better than all the rest—but he would make me a better person by enabling me to be more of the person that I am.

And that's just what I'm becoming.

A New Beginning

There was a short time in my life when I got tired of seeing all of the wedding and baby pictures pop up in my News Feed. Thankfully, that time only lasted about two weeks and then I was over it. And it happened years ago.

Whew…I'm glad I'm not like that anymore. That's such self-entitlement to feel that way. "I deserve this…why do they have that?" It's serious jealousy and anybody who says otherwise isn't being truthful with themselves.

Now I relish in the fact that my friends are in happy, meaningful relationships. I get the whole *wanting to take lots of pictures and post them* thing now. It isn't to make other people envious or spiteful. No, it's because the happiness is literally overwhelming. And I have felt that feeling after having met Matthew. I want to gush and plaster it every which way that I can. I want to post quotes of mushy stuff and upload pictures of the two of us and just be goofy with it all because I honestly can't stop smiling.

I've reached the point where that corniness just comes out, and I don't care at all what other people think. I start to notice myself doing and saying things that I never thought were possible for me to do. That level of comfort is not always a real place for some people. Only the ones who let themselves go there get to have that.

And I think that's one of the greatest places to ever be.

So bring on the pictures, friends. You can even post what you ate with your significant other last night. Or the flowers that he bought you for the third time in the last week. Or the baby food all over your child's face that looks like throw-up. I want it all, because it means that you're living. You're just going to have to deal with mine, too.

P.S. Maybe Matthew will finally take me to Medieval Times for a photo op!

What the Future Holds

I'm not sure what the future holds for Matthew and I. My life drastically changed in those ten dates. When I started falling, I never stropped, and it's been a fun ride. There have been ups and downs, but the slopes are what brought us to these hills.

Don't ever fool yourself into thinking that good couples don't have problems or argue. That's just life. Don't buy into the notion that disagreements can't happen. They do. It is in these moments that your character and love for one another is defined. How are you going to act? What are you going to say? How are you going to say it? Are you going to quit? Can you hold hands even while you're fuming? It took me a while to understand that arguments are inevitable, but that I can be a part of the solution. It wasn't until that realization that our communication got much better, and Matthew and I became a team instead of opponents.

So, while I'm not sure what my future holds, regardless of how great things have been and how we've managed to conquer the down times, what I do know is these ten dates have led to nearly seven months of early morning texts, surprise flowers, early trips home (just to see me), and countless kisses that I wouldn't trade for a thing.

Maybe I'm not supposed to know how things will end up. Maybe Matthew came as a surprise, so perhaps my journey should be a surprise, too. Besides, is it really about the destination, or rather, who you're with on the journey?

My life will forever be changed.

Part 3: Lessons Learned

I Am Not Finished

In therapy, we often talk about three things that are all very similar in the curative sense: universality, catharsis, and troubles talk. Universality means that your troubles are not just your own. Catharsis is the emotional release of those feelings, and troubles talk combines the two: you release your emotional troubles and feelings with someone who shares those similarities with you.

As I mentioned at the very beginning, you are not alone. You are normal. I can attest to that. I've been there with you. What you're about to read is what I learned along the way to finding love. Whatever it is—sentimental or humorous—it was my journey. And that's the most valuable lesson I learned throughout this process. I learned that this is mine. And it is pieces of my journey, not my destination.

I am not finished.

19

Online Etiquette

Perceptions

Life is all about perception. What we make of the world is based on what we take away from it as our own reality.

I changed my profile picture on Facebook today. Previously, it was Matthew and I on a cliff in California, overlooking the ocean. Today, it was me on a cliff in California, overlooking the ocean. You can imagine what that looked like to my Facebook world. I received several phone calls, texts, and messages, asking if I was okay. Needless to say, I have the greatest friends. But, there was nothing to worry about. So, if perception is reality, how do we face the *real* facts if our perception isn't totally on point with the truth?

Doesn't this sort of thing happen often? *My girlfriend is constantly playing on Pinterest; she must be bored with me. My boyfriend loves to watch football; he must not like me as much. Christie changed her profile picture; there must be trouble in paradise.* Trust me, I'm sometimes guilty of these thought patterns, too.

But, ask yourself: Does your girlfriend playing on Pinterest really equate to her not liking you? Does your boyfriend's interest in football mean he's bored with you? Or is it possible that she simply likes Pinterest, and he likes football?

So, next time your guy or girl wonders about something like Pinterest or football because they love you enough to care, try not to take offense. Instead, take it as a compliment.

Looks like my original profile picture is back. I like it better anyways. It looked like I was missing something by my side in the other. I'd say I was.

The Selfie

Oh, the dreaded, shirtless, self-body shots taken in a mirror. Preferably with abs that look like they've been doused in baby oil and Photoshopped on. The kissy-faced selfies in a car with a caption that reads, "On my way to work!" (Don't we all go to work?)

Seeing these almost causes me real, somatic pain as I observe them in all their hashtag glory. Girls are definitely guilty of the selfies, but guys are, too. I've seen more tattoos in places that I didn't even know existed all because of these #gympics. And the flexing. It kills me. Because it's so natural to be seen with bulging biceps positioned in an L-shape in the air?

So, yes, we've all seen some selfies in our day, but apparently we have not all observed the text strands between friends outlining the disgust that follows. This seems especially true if you're the culprit of these pictures. You're likely oblivious these messages even exist.

To demonstrate, I received a text and a picture from a girlfriend the other day who wrote, "Can you believe this guy made this shirtless selfie his Facebook profile picture? I've never seen somebody so full of himself." We get it. You work out. Just like the gals out there putting their solo bathing suit pictures up front and center. Sure, you have time to run and you've got a hot body because of it.

The reason this is so annoying is not because we're jealous. (The friend that sent me that text is a size 0 and 100 pounds. She is outrageously beautiful.) No, the reason is because it doesn't benefit anyone. It serves the person posting the picture and does nothing positive for anyone seeing it.

Ok, I get it, boys. Yeah, it's eye-candy to see a cute girl in a bikini. But, pick up a magazine with airbrushed pics and it'll serve the same purpose, without the brag, if that's what you're looking for.

So, before you go posting another #fakecandidselfie, think about the repercussionary (I made that word up) texts and thoughts by those people you want to see your pictures. And if you want to be a good friend, tell your pals to stop.

How to Lose a Guy (or Girl) 101.

Musturbation

Yes, you read the title correctly. (Get your head out of the gutter, at least for now. Hold your breath until the end.) It's a real term used in the counseling field. It was coined by one of the most influential psychologists of all time, Albert Ellis, who founded Rational Emotive Behavior Therapy (REBT). Ellis believed that often times, psychosis can be caused by irrational thought patterns.

So, what is musturbation?

Musturbation is an irrational thought pattern that refers to the "must" and "should" conditions that we place on ourselves, others, and the world. These musturbation thought patterns may sound like, "I should be," "You must be," and "The world ought to be."

So, why am I talking about this?

Because of masturbation. Yep. Now your head can be in the gutter for a second. A few days ago I received a series of text messages from a guy that I went on a few dates with a long time ago. The subject? Masturbation. I thought I'd lay out these texts for you as a *you-must-never-do-this-to-anyone-ever* kind of thing.

So, here goes:
Icky: *"I just got home from a date."*
Me: *"How did it go?"*
Icky: *"She wasn't really for me."*
Me: *"Why not?"*
Icky: *"Maybe not as confident as I need?"*
Me: *"Okay, tell me more."*
Icky: *"Perhaps it was because I was thinking about you the whole time I was out with her?"*
Me: *"Shut up."*
Icky: *"That weird?"*
Me: *"Go to bed."*
Icky: *"I am in bed. And you know what that means!"* (Insert hand gesture emoticon with two water splash emoticons following it.)
Me: (Silence.)

The next morning at 7:57 a.m.

Icky: *"I was messin' with you last night about the whole thinkin' about you during my date thing. I figured you had picked up on that, but I'm clarifying just in case. Although, you do often pop in my head when I'm masturbating."*
Me: (Silence.)

That evening at 9:44 p.m.

Icky: *"Too much?"*

Me: (Silence.)

10:27 p.m.

Icky: *"Christie!! I was only tryin' to get a rise out of ya!!!"*

And again...
Me: (Silence.)

So, not only did he deliver one of the ickiest messages that I've ever received, but he attempted to retract what he said the following day by saying, "I was messin' with you," and then he retracted the retraction by stating, "Although you do often pop in my head when I'm..."

I feel dizzy with all of those spins.

Let me just say... If you're having thought patterns like "I ought not to send text messages to unsuspecting individuals regarding my masturbatory thoughts," that is *not* musturbation.

You *must not* send those messages.

The Justification Text

Everyone knows what the *justification text* is. It's the (ineffective) quicksand move. You know...you get stuck in something, realize it, and panic. Instead of easing your way out, you rush to escape and basically create your own self-destruction. It's the message that you give or receive shortly after a conversation as a means to compensate for what was just said or done that didn't sit well with the recipient.

I got one of those texts from the "musturbation" guy.

This fella felt the need to justify his message to me about his masturbatory thoughts by being a scientist. This is how it went...

> Bill Nye: "Christie, as far as science goes, a man cannot help what pops into his head during masturbation."
>
> Me: "So, you're (still) admitting that you think of me?"
>
> Bill Nye: "Yes. You do pop into my head often. It is what it is. It literally can't be helped. I'll be sure to slap myself next time you pop in."
>
> Me: "I guess you can't help who you think about when you masturbate, but you can help not texting a girl about it."
>
> Bill Nye: "Men and women masturbate, Christie. Nothing wrong with it."
>
> Me: "Why are you sharing it with me??"
>
> Bill Nye: "I'm not anymore. Just talking science at this point. I don't know why you're implying that I'm gross. Do you call your patients gross if they talk about masturbation?"
>
> Me: "My patients don't tell me that they think about me when they masturbate."

And that, my friends, is the *justification text*. Stupidity.

It's science.

YGWYWM

See how quickly you judged that title? According to psychologist Malcolm Gladwell in the book, *Blink*, you judged the title based on your *adaptive unconscious*. The adaptive unconscious is your brain's ability to make split-second judgments about somebody or something without even knowing it.

Ok, so you judged my title. No offense taken. But, what it stands for is this: You're Gonna Wish You Were Mine. I have utilized the YGWYWM-smile as well as the YGWYWM-text. Both have been empirically tested (of course only by myself and my friends), and both have proven to be effective in various domains—not only with our exes, but with haters, too.

The premise behind this particular type of smile or text is that they are unwarranted. The person receiving this happy-go-lucky smile accompanied by a possible wave or hug does not deserve to be smiled at or embraced so warmly.

A perfect text example would go a little something like this:

Jerk ex-boyfriend: *"Hey. It was good to see you today. Hope you are doing well."*

Awesome You: *"Hey! Good seein' you, too! Gotta run, but have a great day!"*

You were joyful when he didn't anticipate it. You were unexpectedly short and to the point. And you maintained control by ending it, which probably confused your ex.

YGWYWM.

Sure, this may be deemed passive-aggressive, but you have to understand one thing about this concept: The smile and the text are not for the recipient. They are for *you*.

How so?
1. You just recognized your worth by maintaining the notion that someone should want *you*.
2. You turned a negative situation into a positive one by confronting an inevitable nightmare.
3. You maintained control of yourself.
4. You finished whatever you were doing with a smile.

How many times did you read the pronouns *they*, *he*, or *she* in the above-mentioned list? Not once. It was about *you*.

So, keep that smile going and direct it towards someone who wants to give it back. Maybe find someone who YGWT.

(You're Gonna Want, Too.)

Grammer Count's To

I hope when you read this title you got as irked as I did writing it. So, a little disclosure... I used to be a third grade special education teacher. But, I promise this does not make me any more of a Grammar Policewoman than the other girls I know.

Immediately after I receive a text from a guy, my smart and adorably sassy (former) roommate will ask how he spelled the word *your*. A quick and easy way to lose (not to be confused with "loose") a girl in ten is to look like a bozo. If you're capable of a spoken word, then surely you're capable of a written one, especially since we're moving in that direction with our incessant texting. (Totally guilty, by the way.)

As cute as you may be, you are no exception to the rule. Looks fade with time. It'd be nice to have your brain intact as we get older. So, I thought I'd help you with a fast food lesson on some of the grammar basics that annoy many of us girls:

1. Too = also
2. Smooshing words together = contractions. Get to know these little guys. They will become your best friends. Pretend that the apostrophe is a Band-Aid connecting two words together (e.g., have + not = haven't). The most common mistakes are *your* vs. *you're*, *its* vs. *it's*, and *were* vs. *we're*.

3. Learn the difference between *then* and *than*. *Then* is mainly an adverb typically used with time, and *than* is a conjunction used mostly to make comparisons.
4. Believe it or not, *there*, *their*, and *they're* are also different words. Seriously.
5. Google should become your new go-to buddy when in writing mechanics doubt.

The following is a horrific text example: *"im going too the store later if your in the mood than lets eat christie"*

Good heavens—please don't eat me!!

What could have worked is this: *"I'm going to the store later. If you're in the mood, then let's eat, Christie."*

The capital letters used to begin the sentences and make my name a proper noun were appreciated. Likewise, the contractions, commas, periods, and appropriate uses of the words *then* and *to* were also noted. Nice work. I officially like you based on your writing alone.

20
Lessons From Strangers

Cray

I can't tell you how many times I've heard the phrase, "I swear I'm not crazy."

I was out the other day shopping at Lenox Mall in Atlanta, and lo and behold, I met a guy. He was sitting in the middle of the mall at the Starbucks across from J.Crew. (I really need to find a new locale.) As I finished ordering my white chocolate mocha with one and a half shots of espresso and five pumps of white mocha (less caffeine, extra sugar—yes, I do realize what I'm ordering), he approached me as I was walking away. He commented on my heels and inquired about how I managed to walk in them. I wanted to ask him how he walked in his loafers. I didn't understand the question.
"Umm...one foot in front of the other?"
He continued to walk with me as I was heading to Bloomingdale's. (Guys, don't do that. Do I really need to explain why?) I told him that I was in a hurry and it was nice to meet him, but that I had to go. This is similar to when a girl tells a guy at a bar that she isn't a good dancer. (This means that she doesn't want to dance with you. Think about it, if you were the right guy, she'd dance terribly for you.) He realized my haste, so of course he pressed further. He proceeded to

tell me that he was just a "normal" guy and that I seemed like a "cool" girl, and he just wanted to talk. I shrugged my shoulders, half-grinned, and said, "Well, thanks. That's sweet."

And then Crazy Pants had to take it to the next level.

"Look, I'm not crazy. I just want to get to know you. You seem really interesting."

Case in point. You told me you were crazy by telling me that you are *not* crazy. It's like saying, "I swear I don't have a big massive zit on my face." Why would you say it if you didn't think there could be a huge boulder on your cheek?

And so I end with one of my favorite Match.com emails: "Wow, so Atlanta is where the Lord keeps His angels hiding out. What would it take to put a smile on your face and get you off the market? I'm hoping I can snatch you up before some of those no-gooders get you, lol. Well, in time, I'd love to be the one putting a ring on your finger IF your personality matches your beauty. I hope it does. Please don't turn into a monster on me, lol. I don't need any more of those. And don't worry, I'm not one of those Crazies, lol."

'Nuff said.

My Lesbian Moment

If you haven't been approached by the same sex yet, I have to tell you...it's a little flattering. I don't know why, but it just is. Or, was.

It just happened to me.

I was standing in line at a barbeque restaurant waiting for my take-out order of roasted chicken, meatloaf, broccoli casserole, and mashed potatoes and gravy. (Maybe that's where I got the gal. I can certainly eat and have no shame in the matter.) As I was waiting by the door, standing next to a handsome, ringless gentleman whom I was adamantly ignoring, I suspect that the store manager gal interpreted my behavior as dodgy and assumed I was not interested in men. I mean, the guy was a stud. The kind that you'd probably stare at in a magazine for a solid five minutes and tell your boyfriend that you really like his "outfit" because you want an excuse to look longer.

What reason would I have to ignore him? Except for the fact that I hadn't washed my hair, didn't have an ounce of makeup on, and likely smelled like a farm because I was returning home from seeing a client in the boonies, I had no reason to ignore him.

Perhaps the gal gives me more credit than I give myself. Thank you for your sweetness. But, I have to give it to her, she was quite perceptive of my behavior. I started to notice that she kept eye-balling me and smiling at every chance she had. The only reason I was looking back was because I was famished and eager to get my food and head home. When she asked if I wanted plastic silverware and butter, I replied, "Yes to the butter, no to the silverware. I'll try to help out the environment a little bit while I'm killing my body. It'll be a good tradeoff."

She laughed for way too long.

Then, she told me that she liked that. The environmental thoughtfulness, that is. As she handed me my bag and I was about to dart to my car in the hopes that I wouldn't eat my fingers off on the way, she asked me where I like to hang out. I told her that I usually stick to Buckhead but have been a little tired of it lately. (That's my response at any given time to anyone.) She proceeded to ask if I've ever been to My Sister's Room over in Grant Park, to which I replied, "No, that doesn't sound familiar. I don't think I have." (I'm too new to Atlanta to know what that is.)

And then she dropped it. The bomb.

"Well, if you ever want to go with me sometime, I'd love to take you." And my dumb response: "Oh yeah, sure. I know where to find you!"

Immediately upon leaving the restaurant and climbing into my Jeep, I no longer felt hungry. My new mission was not to fill my belly, but to find out what exactly My Sister's Room is. And sure enough, you guessed it. (Thank God for smart phones.)

This experience got me thinking about who we fall in love with and whether we have a choice in the matter. Can you really help who you like? Or are we naturally drawn to a certain kind of person over another? And, if you have to force yourself out of love with someone, is it authentic? I know that I've felt very deeply for people in my past. Sure, those feelings have dissipated now, but at the time, they were very real. And if you had asked me at the time if I could somehow magically turn those feelings off with a switch, I know I wouldn't have been able to do it. I'm thankful I haven't been denied the greatest gift that we have in this life, the one that most people get to freely experience: Love.

And, besides, I'm flattered by my new lesbian friend.

Speeding Ticket Reduction

I got a speeding ticket the other day. It was totally my fault. I was returning home from a root canal, and I was going 78 mph in a 55 zone. Irresponsible. I was swollen, tired, and ready to be home. And now, on top of the cost to fix my tooth, I had to pay an extra fee for speeding. But as much as I'm complaining, I shouldn't be. I was shown some grace along the way.

The officer that clocked me reduced my speed so that I wouldn't accrue any points on my license. The reason: Because I acknowledged that it was my fault. I told him that I was speeding because I was attempting to get home due to my miserable mouth pain.

The officer looked at me and said, "So, you know how fast you were going?" And I said, "Yes, sir. I was definitely speeding and I shouldn't have been. I just wanted to get home to rest, but that's no excuse." He ran my license, brought back the reduced speeding ticket, and with a smile, said, "Thank you for being honest."

So, yeah, sure...I still got a speeding ticket, which wasn't the best icing on my cake, but, admitting fault worked to my benefit in *some* way. And it got me thinking that if more relationships operated like this, those not-so-good times could be reduced, just like my ticket.

No one expects their significant other to be perfect all the time. But, what many *do* expect is an admittance of a mistake. To let someone know that you didn't *actually* mean what you did; that there was no ill will or malice behind the actions. It's okay to give an explanation for why something was done. In fact, *please* do that. But then you need to back it up with a sincere apology.

We'll never be perfect. But, by acknowledging that we're not, we're communicating something that *is* perfect: humility and empathy.

Bump

My two longest relationships (other than my family) involve my two best friends, Molly and Christine. I met Molly in the 2nd grade and Christine in the 4th grade. It's hard to put into words how much they mean to me. The three of us took a trip to Boston a few years ago, and on this trip I did more walking than I've ever done in my life. On one of those strolls, I got a bit chilly because I was in a silky tank top, so I needed to buy something to keep me warm.

First, you need to know that I have what you would call the *kid-in-a-candy-store syndrome*. My favorite shoes in the entire world are Jack Rogers Navajo sandals. They're nothing special, but I love them. And I have about 20 pair, some are even duplicates of the same color. I have a heyday when I fall in love with an item and I tend to overbuy. (My mother can attest to this with serious anxiety.)

On this Boston trip, my disorder got the best of me...again. I got not one, not two, but three Harvard shirts—a t-shirt, a long sleeve t-shirt, and a sweatshirt—just in case I needed a variety of lengths. Yes, you read that correctly...Harvard. Why? Because it's right there, and Boston seems to cater to us syndromed folk, so their apparel was all over the city.

So, just the other day, back in Atlanta, I decided to sport my Harvard sweatshirt because it was raining outside and I couldn't find my hooded jacket. I needed a break from writing, so I took a short walk in my neighborhood to decompress.

On this walk, I met a guy...

We bumped into each other.

Literally.

I was listening to music and texting at the same time—a dangerous combination—and I walked straight into him as he was heading toward me. Thankfully, he got a good chuckle out of my absent-mindedness, and so he began walking with me. (I'm just now realizing how strange it was that we took a walk together.) After our short encounter, he ended on, "So, did you go to Harvard?" I desperately wanted to say "yes" in the most nonchalant, overly arrogant way that I could, just to seem uber smart; however, I resisted the urge. I laughed, looked down at my half-bleached, once maroon hoodie, and said, "Nope, I just got cold one day." The guy laughed and said, "Well, good, because then I'd be too intimidated to talk to you."

Okay, wait, he was talking to me based on the *assumption* that I did *not* go to Harvard? If that's supposed to flatter me, he did a really poor job. And if I *had* gone to Harvard, he wouldn't continue talking to me? I don't get it. Don't we want to be with somebody who challenges us? Why would somebody's job or educational background intimidate us to the point that we wouldn't talk to them? Likewise, was he admitting that he's dumb? Or at least not up to intellectual par? Interesting.

P.S. Beware of girls who walk and text. May cause injury.

...Or maybe *don't* beware of girls walking and texting so that you *can* bump into them.

Just make sure they didn't go to Harvard.

Virgin on Plane

My girlfriend, Chelsey, and I traveled from Ohio to Florida for a mini girl's trip a few years ago. On our way home, our plane literally caught on fire mid-flight. I'm not kidding...the cabin filled with smoke, the flight attendant rushed to the front of the plane and strapped herself into the seat facing us, and she had panic written all over. Chelsey and I just looked at each other and laughed. Over the speaker, the pilot indicated that there was a "small fire" on the plane, and reported that we were going to have to turn back around for an emergency landing. We had only been in the air for 15 minutes, so all we had to do was make a quick loop in the sky to land back on our original runway.

We still, to this day, have no idea why our reaction was full of laughter as our plane was on fire in the sky with us on it. Perhaps it seemed too surreal. At one point, I distinctly remember turning to Chelsey and saying, "Well, take a good look around because we'll probably be seeing these people in Heaven tonight!" And we continued to laugh uncontrollably. Within those few minutes of turning around, I had the insight to call my mom and dad to say my final "goodbye." (Remember: We weren't far off the ground, so I was still able to get cell phone reception.) Against the airline's rules, I made the call and we spoke for a few minutes. I don't really remember the conversation, but I remember my very unrelated thought afterward:

I'm still a virgin.

I was one month shy of graduating from college and I had been waiting just like my mom had when she was close to my age. I always thought that I wanted to be in love and to wait for the right person. Besides, the best things in life require patience, right? I heard it put so perfectly the other night from a guy at a bar talking about *not* cheating on his girlfriend (of all things)... When his one guy friend observed a girl attempting to talk to this gentleman, he turned to him and said, "Dude, she's hot, why are you not talking to her?" And his reply was, "Because of (insert name). I don't say 'no' to the whiskey because I don't want the drink." So, of course he wants attention from this girl, and honestly, he probably wouldn't hate sleeping with her either. She *was* hot. But maybe he has another drink that tastes just as good and he doesn't want to jump to the next one all because it *might* be better. What if it tastes like crap? Holding out for things that seem to be worth it are often worth it, like this girl apparently was to him. I proceeded to embrace this guy at the bar and told him how wonderful he was.

And *that's* how to win a girl!

You're Driving Me Nuts

A few nights ago, I hung out with several people—only one of whom I knew. In the group was a guy that I had just met. He drove me absolutely nuts. From the moment I walked in to his house where everyone was gathering before going out, he began harpooning me (in a joking way) about everything. It had been a while since I'd been able to dish it back to someone, so I took full advantage and cut up with him. I can't remember specifically what we talked about because there were honestly so many things that were touched upon, but I remember the overall feeling of being exceedingly annoyed...in kind of a good way.

There's this concept in psychology called the *sleeper effect*. Research shows that often times, a message does not resonate with someone until after some length of time has passed, and quite frequently, the *source* of the message is forgotten. That's kind of what happened here.

As I'm looking back on that brief interaction, I don't really remember the source of the message, and I don't even truly recall the message itself, but I am acutely aware of the lingering feeling that I am left with. And honestly, that feeling is something that I missed as a single girl. As ironic as it may seem, it kind of feels good knowing that someone has enough of an impact on your life to disrupt it.

I've met several people who have gotten under my skin at first, but eventually their idiosyncrasies didn't bug me anymore. That's part of the reason why I love Matthew. He can irk me enough to keep me on my toes every now and then, which is an indication that I truly care enough to allow him to have that effect on me.

So, if you're in a relationship and feel like you want to pull all your hair out, maybe it's not *such* a terrible thing? After all, Cameron Diaz didn't look all that bad in *My Sister's Keeper*.

21

Lessons From My Friends

Gumption

Did I mention that the book you're reading started as an innocent dating blog? Well, I inevitably got a lot of feedback regarding my blog. It's true, you can't write about the do's and don'ts of dating without getting critiqued every once in a while. Most of my friends were more than on board. In fact, many jumped on the ship and it sailed before I knew it. But others, namely family members and protective guy friends, were worried about my impending dating doom following each post. They would ask, "Christie, do you ever expect to date anybody after blogging about this sort of thing?!" I'm fairly certain that many of these loving individuals sat in angst with clenched stomachs until I made my next post, waiting to see if I said something totally off the wall. (Apparently I have a tendency to be pretty uninhibited in my regular, "real" life, so I don't blame them for worrying.) Nevertheless, I wrote. And let me just say, you'd be surprised about those dating doom assumptions.

One of my favorite after-effects of my blog was my newly acquired pen pal via Facebook. He's a pseudo-friend from my big high school. I say "pseudo" because we don't actually remember each other. We have hundreds of mutual friends and seemingly several things in common; however, the origin of our existence is a vague memory.

At the beginning of this rekindled friendship flame, Pen Pal Facebook Friend sent me an "atta boy" message of encouragement, telling me that he was reading my blog and enjoying it. Since then, we messaged back and forth and even became CPO (cell phone official). During this time, I realized one thing: PPFF has mastered a trait that has long been forgotten. He has gumption.

Through heartaches and sadness, people tend to lose their ability to have enough confidence to do the things they want to do. They forget what it feels like to be a young kid who thinks he can fly if he wraps a beach towel around his shoulders and jumps high enough. But not PPFF. As intimidating as it may have been to message a girl who was writing a blog about the guys she encounters, he still reached out. And I'll say...that confidence is the most attractive trait that we have as human beings.

So, as my dad would say, "Grow a pair." And I say, "Start living your life the way you want to." What do you have to lose if you don't already have it?

A Picture is Worth a Thousand Slideshows

When I was going on lots of dates as a single girl, I started this *thing* with a guy where I would send him slideshows of pictures with captions via text. Sometimes I just get bored, especially if I was sitting at a table full of people who were texting other people instead of having a conversation with one another. So, I started this because it was not only entertaining for him (I hope), but it was loads of fun for me. I found myself laughing out loud and then being asked what my textee sent that made me chuckle. Whether he wanted to receive them or not, he got them.

So one day, after sending yet another captioned slideshow, I asked if this whole *slideshow-texting-thing* is something that "wins" a guy. (I had to ask because I honestly didn't know if he actually *liked* receiving my texts.) According to him, the slideshow "works." It shows him that I care enough to take the time to send pictures, and it includes him in my life and memories.

It's so simple to try. Just pick out roughly ten pictures—mostly goofy—and under each one, describe the picture. And send. Simple as that! They're super fun to receive, too.

I can definitely say they'd "win" me over. You might just have to increase your cellular data plan, though.

Have fun!!

Cougar Town

I recently went to the St. Regis with some friends to meet up with a buddy. When we arrived, my friend was being attacked by a cougar. The lady had to have been in her early 50s and my friend is a young buck in his late 20s. Sitting on the sofa, inching his way to the corner near the armrest, the cougar kept leaning in completely disregarding my presence along with anybody else's. She proceeded to take pictures of just him on her iPhone, to which she uploaded to Instagram immediately. I'm sure this lil' lady wanted to show off the fact that she was hanging out with such a young lad.

In a Chico's version of the BCBG bandage dress with uncrossed legs, we could see all that she had on underneath. (Let's keep a little mystery alive, shall we girls?) Her skin was pulled back behind her ears, and her lips were fuller than Joan Rivers'. Honestly, she'd probably be stunning if she'd just be her normal self.

While the woman was showing off her photography skills, my friend noticed that my jaw was on the floor. In order to pick it back up, he texted me at arms-length away and said, *"I am being cougar-attacked."*

Now, up until this point, I was unaware that my friend didn't know this cougar. He appeared to know her *very* well. Once I found this little fact out, all bets were off and I began working my magic.

I leaned in to "Ms. Trixie" (that's what her name sounded like slurred) and told her that my friend was recently single (not true) and that he was particularly fragile at this time in his life (not true), and that he needed some TLC (also not true). Getting death stares from my guy friend, I proceeded to ask her what she did and where she lived, to which neither of those she could answer. When you weigh close to nothing, it takes nearly nothing to cause inebriation. I'm guessing she was close to blacking out by this point and I quickly got over our short-lived love.

But, before I left, I told Ms. Trixie that my friend was actually my boyfriend and that I was just teasing her. (I'm not that cruel to where I'd leave him totally in the dust.) She must have thought I was speaking Latin because she appeared to not understand a word that I said. And then I got fed up and left through an Irish Exit. Shortly thereafter, my friend followed.

I'm guessing they broke up.

So, a few things in regards to dating/not dating a cougar:
1. Always, always, always take up any opportunity to entertain a cougar whether you plan to date the person or not. It's just way too fun and completely free for all bar ages.
2. Don't ever admit to someone (like me) that you're being attacked by a cougar, because then *we'll* seize that opportunity for you.
3. If you're being called "Miss" or "Sir," know that those around you view you as... well...old.

4. If you're a cougar, don't try to *not* look like a cougar. It only makes you look like more of one.
5. If you're interested in a cougar, don't try to hide her age. We all likely possess that special ability those carnival workers have at guessing ages.

Meow.

Why Me?

I was talking to a girlfriend on the phone the other day. She was upset. The guy that she likes isn't paying her the kind of attention she deserves. She told me that she seems to like him more than he likes her. Through tears, we processed through the *what* and *how* of her feelings...not so much the *why*. Why not the *why*? Because it doesn't really matter. Is she willing to change who she is? No. Nor should she. So, getting into the *why* of him not paying her attention isn't relevant. We went deeper and discussed the reality of him possibly not liking her. I know that may seem like a harsh thing to do, but it's only preparing her for a potential heartache.

This sweet girl reported that she would feel a sense of loss if he didn't like her. She said that he brings a smile to her face and makes her a happier person. If things suddenly ended, my friend would experience incredible pain because he adds something to her life.

So, I went through a series of simple-to-ask, hard-to-answer questions:
1. Is he the kind of person that you think there should be more of in the world?
2. Would you want your kids to be like him or would you want them to be different?
3. What would *he* be missing if he lost *you*?

Let's focus on #3 for a moment. Why do we, especially us girls, constantly focus on what *we'd* be losing if we didn't end up with the guy that we like? What, really, would we be missing? Companionship? We can find that with someone else. Fun? Lots of people are fun. Smiles? Something as simple as a funny movie can make us smile. So, are they really the end-all, be-all? What about their heart do you love? Do you admire them? *We* have so much to offer.

So, why all the worry? Because you're afraid you'll experience heartache? Haven't most people? You don't have time to worry. With the time that you're spending worrying, you could be out enjoying somebody else's company. You've got to change your self-talk into something affirming. Why would anyone expect to see your incredible traits if you don't?

It's *your* life. Not somebody else's. Make yourself smile since that's all you can control. Don't wait on a guy to make you happy. And if you can't seem to put a smile on your own face, do what I always tell my girlfriends to do when they're sad... Make somebody else happy! Seriously—it will bring a smile to your face. Guaranteed.

On that note, I'm about to go buy a coffee for an unsuspecting patron!

We Were on a Break

My blog and I went on a "break." I had taken over a month to write. Life got a little busy. In that time, I started to wonder if the old saying "absence makes the heart grow fonder" was, in fact, really true.

I've heard my friends talk about wanting to "take a break" from their significant others to create those "missing" feelings again. You know, to spark some sort of passion that they feel is lacking. But by doing this, they are essentially saying to each other, "I like you, but I cannot stand to be around you right now... I need a break from you." Anybody who wants a break from you doesn't want to be with you. End of story. (Literally.)

Oh sure, stay with a guy that wants to see if there's somebody better for him out there because he's not completely satisfied with you. If he comes back, are you honestly flattered?

And don't kid yourself... By being away from my blog, I didn't once feel like I was really missing it. I was busy. Great things filled my time. And in that time, I just got used to not writing. I think the same goes for relationships. You learn to live without someone when you are apart from them. Sure, in the beginning, the pain can really sting. But, if you're going to *intentionally* take time apart in order to miss someone, that means that you'll be sticking it out through those initial stings. Which means that you'll *force* yourself not to call or visit the person so that you can "miss them." But this really only causes you to get used to not being with the person. Thankfully we have that ability as humans. For example, if a loved one passes away or falls out of love with us, our hearts eventually heal and we can move on.

Yes, when I went back into action with my blog, I was thankful to be writing again. It's therapeutic for me. But, it's frustrating and annoying trying to get back into the "writing mode" when it doesn't feel natural anymore. My blog very easily could have ended following my break.

So, my advice is simple: If you want to be apart from someone, there's a reason. Taking time apart in order to create a new love for that same person is a trick of the mind that doesn't work. And, frankly, it's just weird. Just break up. That's what "I want a break" equates to. You're doing yourself a big favor if you laugh and move on.

And when he tells his friends that you're probably sitting around sulking, laugh even harder.

Bodily Sprint

There's a picture of my best girlfriend and I from when we were in the 4th grade that's been circulating around (my world of) Facebook. The reason: Because it's absolutely ridiculous. It was pre-hair straightener days when holding a fake gun to the air like you were one of Charlie's Angels was cool. The comments from my newer Facebook friends who know the both of us have already started about how surprising it is to see me taller than her. (Of all the comedic gold that could be found in that picture, *that* was what they latched on to?)

What they don't realize is that I've been pretty much the same size since the 4th grade. Yes, puberty hit early and I sprouted up fast. I was the "tall" girl then. But, it stopped there. These days, I am not well-endowed. I don't have nice, womanly curves. I look like an adolescent boy. I just grew faster than the others, and then they caught up. Instead of being on a marathon, my body went on a sprint. (Possibly a stroll.)

I often find myself still feeling like I did when I was in the 4th grade. I'm the loud, short girl who thinks I'm just as tall as everybody else. And the reason I feel this way is because I'm holding on to a lot of old feelings.

I view myself now as I was back then.

I'll go shopping and look at a pair of extra-long jeans that (obviously) won't fit, but to my eyes, they look just right. It isn't until I try them on that I realize I literally need to have about two feet taken off the length.

Likewise, I have a friend who lost a lot of weight in her adult years. When she was younger, she wasn't as in charge of her health as she is now. Her body has changed.

Sometimes, I hear her say that she could never wear something that she could very easily (and beautifully) wear today.

I think this old way of thinking can affect our relationships, too, when we view ourselves by the past rather than living in the present. It can also affect who we choose to be with because, sometimes, we can't get over the past.

The phrase, "people who live in glass houses shouldn't throw stones," definitely applies to me right now. I'll be the first to admit that an ex's past definitely helped define my outlook on who he was. Mentally, I couldn't get over the fact that he had cheated on his past girlfriend. It bothered me and I judged him not with words, but with actions. I was overly cautious and guarded my heart by not letting him in, so as to not get hurt or cheated on.

But, is that fair to do?

I've heard the phrase, "once a cheater, always a cheater," but I have to disagree. (My opinion is very subjective, so take it with a grain of salt if you like.) I can muster up a few logical statements and questions in regard to this notion that even cheaters can change:

1. I wouldn't be in the mental health profession, and I wouldn't have devoted all this time and (educational) energy to my career, if I didn't believe that people could change.
2. Lots of people wouldn't be in my career field if they didn't think that it was possible for people to mature.
3. Have you ever changed?
4. Why would it be impossible for other people to grow and change, too?

There's no reason to live in the past if we're in the present right now. Doesn't the present serve a purpose? Call me naïve, but unless it relates to me, I don't need to know what a guy has done in the past. I believe people can change.

Just be thankful that whatever he chose to do then, brought him to you now.

One Sentence

Why is it so hard to be still?

I told one of my best friends that I've been having trouble sleeping because it's difficult for me to rest when I know that I need to be working more. I *just* finished graduate school, and my entire life I've made one plan after the next. And this time, I don't have a plan. I'm looking for one.

Since I was five years old, I've always been on the go, creating agendas for my life. I'm almost 30 and I've been married to the educational system this entire time. (It's been my longest relationship.) And when I'm not in school, I'm working, or looking for work. When I'm working, I'm looking to advance my career through some sort of promotion. If I'm not in a relationship, I'm looking for one. If I'm in a relationship, I'm thinking about the next step. If I were married, I'm sure I'd be thinking about when I'd be having kids. If I had kids, I'm positive I'd be pondering where they should go to school.

Why do we do this to ourselves? Why do I feel guilty that I'm at sort of a (healthy) impasse right now? What's the rush?

I'm going to Europe soon on holiday (yeah, I said "holiday"). Maybe it's okay that I take a break for a second so I can breathe. Maybe I should enjoy my vacation. Besides, it's my way of celebrating the fact that I graduated! Rather than worry myself sick about where and when and how and why I'm going to take X job, and move to X place because it makes X sense, perhaps I should focus on the blessing that not having all those X's really is.

It starts with gratitude. If we are grateful for what we have, will we really be focusing so much on what we don't have? With that in mind, I recently started a thankfulness column within my planner. It's one sentence each day about what I'm thankful for. Yesterday, it was devoted to my sweet friend, Katie. By being grateful for her, I wasn't thinking about having to make *more* friends. I was focusing on what I do have with *her*.

One sentence isn't intimidating.

Counting the Joy

I broke down to my friend the other day and shared a really dark time that I experienced several years ago. As you can imagine, it was hard. As it would be for most people to self-disclose like that. This "dark time" involved a serious relationship that had failed. I lost countless friends as a result, all of whom represented something important to me.

It didn't feel good.

Nor did my feelings of worthlessness. Or my loss of hope in life in general. Or the isolation from everything—even from my own thoughts because I was too scared to think them.

I lost a lot of weight. I slept a lot. I dropped out of graduate school for a little while. I struggled to be the person that I was prior to those days. I couldn't be strong enough in my weakness to pick myself up for a little while.

So unlike me now.

In speaking about this to my friend, it was suggested to me that I always appear happy and that I've got it all together. It was a shock that I had ever experienced these kinds of feelings before. And my response was, "Compared to what I went through—the literal hell on Earth that I experienced and wouldn't wish upon anyone, ever—everything else is rainbows and sunshine. I can't help but be happy and thankful to not suffer those feelings anymore."

It got me thinking about the 80/20 rule. Maybe you've heard of it. If you haven't, you are well aware of it because it's, well, life. The rule states that people who are in relationships are generally satisfied 80% of the time (or else they probably wouldn't be with their significant other). But, because nobody is perfect, and therefore, no person can be 100% satisfied with their partner all the time, they stray to find the missing 20%. From what I've observed in life, that 20% is usually mysterious and something foreign. But, it's intriguing, and therefore, enticing.

This rule relates to how I survived during my "dark time," and it's simple: If there isn't a single person that can be 100% satisfying to us all the time, why don't we find that extra 20% within ourselves? Why do we look to other people when we rationally know that they, too, won't be 100% satisfying either? What is it about ourselves that we don't love and can't be happy with?

So, here's the deal: If you're thinking that you can find someone better than who you're with because he or she only fits the bill 80% of the time, I would recommend sticking with that person.

Those 80%'s can be hard to find.

And if you ever feel the way that I did, know that you are not alone. To experience that kind of darkness only means that the light will shine so much brighter someday. When you pick yourself back up, you'll feel like you were wearing sunglasses your whole life and finally took them off. Your eyes will never be the same.

22
Lessons From My Family

Ayden's Smile

I have the most precious nephew. His name is Ayden, and he's in Kindergarten. Ayden and I live very far apart. He's in Ohio and I'm in Georgia. To see each other we use Face Time, thanks to Apple. During one of our recent "visits," my favorite little five-year-old told me about a girl from school. Apparently she's his "girlfriend." Don't you worry, I'll be Googling her in no time. But, before doing so, I had to ask a very basic question that every aunt would inquire.

"Ayden, what does she look like?"

And I was floored by his response. I figured I'd get something like, "She has yellow hair." Or, if he was going to be an extra romantic Kindergartner, he'd say, "She looks pretty." But, instead, my very insightful relative (insert: pride) responded, "She smiles."

I think my heart had an out of body experience and soared up into the heavens for a little bit when I heard that. The depth of that simple response can be so easily overlooked in our adult age. We seem to care more about what we are physically wearing on the outside instead of what we're putting in the inside that will shine through. I've seen a thousand girls dressed in designer clothes without a glimmer of warmth inside of them; walking through bars like they're going to a funeral. Maybe we should all take the time to stop and smile a bit.

Apparently it's how we are perceived, even to children.

Age Makes You Ugly

We're all afraid to age.

Especially us girls.

For whatever reason, we have this idea that aging makes us ugly. We seem to think that the wrinkles on our faces aren't endearing, but are instead revolting. We do everything in our power to diminish them. We worry that, as we grow older, our boyfriends or husbands will no longer think that we are beautiful like they once did.

But, what I think we are unaware of is that we all tend to follow the path of a *dog*. (And no, I don't mean that we look like dogs.) Speaking from past experience, I know what it's like to grow up with a dog. Dogs first begin as puppies, and you can't get enough of them with all of their cuteness. They pee on your floor and you grow a little irritated, but you remain unphased because of the preciousness of that little furball.

Then, in a few months, they become distinguished members of the family with the knowledge of what certain words (err, sounds) mean, and they start to abide by the rules. They grow so fast that you can hardly catch up, and you don't even realize that they don't look like they once did a few months prior unless you compare pictures.

Well, people are like this, too. When I was younger, I distinctly remember a conversation that I had with my Paw-Paw (i.e., granddad). I asked him if he still thought my Maw-Maw was pretty. He chuckled and said, "Of course, sweetheart. Why?" And I explained my prepubescent notion that guys don't like girls who get older because they don't look like they used to. Paw-Paw told me that he hardly notices that Maw-Maw has aged because he grew right along with her. (Sort of like the puppy thing.) And, if anything, she's gotten more beautiful over time because they have grown deeper in their love for one another.

I was an inquisitive little girl, even at that age, so, I inquired further. Without having to probe too much, Paw-Paw put my angst to rest by saying, "Sweetheart, when I see 'pretty' younger girls, they look silly to me. They are too young and I don't find them attractive."

Perhaps guys, even when they're only in their late twenties or thirties, start seeing younger girls like that, too.

Perhaps aging isn't such a bad thing.

Love Letters

I decided to write some short letters. The purpose: Because I have hope. I once heard someone say that you should start planning your future when you're in your twenties. I guess this is my way of planning, just not in the typical sense.

No, I don't have a road map of my life planned out.

No, I don't even have a 401K. (Yikes, I know.)

But, I do have expectations. To love. To have a family; whether I am physically able to have kids or not—I can adopt. To be happy. And it is *because* I am happy right now that I can *plan* to be happy in my future. Because I know how I got here. You've been reading fragments of my life that led to this happiness, and I know I am capable of future happiness, however my life ends up.

So...

To my little girl,

  Be happy. Smile a lot. And find someone who wants to do both of those things with you.

  P.S. You're the reason I've written this book.

To my future husband,

  I loved you before I ever knew you. That's because I loved myself for a long time before I ever met you. And by loving myself, I became more of the person that you love today. Thank you for making me a better person.

  P.S. It's not about me anymore. I get to love you before myself.

To my little boy,

  Act like your daddy. I married him for a reason. Treat your future wife like he treats me.

  P.S. Tell your friends to do the same. And if they don't have great dads like yours, invite them over.

23
Lessons From Matthew

Falling

Even though we use it regularly, the expression, "I've fallen in love" should really be omitted from our vocabulary. The truth is, we should never stop falling. Life should be a long road of tripping every day.

It is in the way he looks at you, and smiles. The way he walks on the side of traffic to protect you, and always tries to make you happy by doing things a little out of the ordinary. When he finishes your sentences to let you know he's listening (*and agreeing*). When he flies home early to see you, and changes his flight to stay longer. When your wants become his wants. When he's proud to introduce you to his family, and asks about your day before he tells you about his. When he always orders a dessert because you love them. When he calls his mom regularly, and holds his grandma's hand when walking in public. When he tries to take care of you by reminding you to get your oil changed and to avoid watching scary movies (so that you're not scared, duh). And, when he doesn't read your blog to learn about you, but instead, *actually* listens to you.

By the end of my life, I plan to be all bruised up.

Yes, these are just a few of the ways.

Be a Miracle to the One You Love

I had a root canal the other day. (If you ever have to go through this painful experience, bring music along with headphones. To say that it's a lifesaver is an understatement.) The day I went under the knife (I love saying that, sounds so much more dramatic than it really was), Matthew postponed his flight to a later time so that he could stay in town and take care of me, and bring me things like Jello and cupcakes.

Unbelievable.

It reminds me of a phrase I once heard: Giving is the best communication. Matthew's actions expressed more to me than any words could have.

Following my *operation* (I hear it was touch-and-go for a while...), I looked like a lop-sided mess. I would try to smile, and the one side of my face would stay still while the other side would go up. It was as if I met a plastic surgeon or a Botox-injector that had it in for me.

Upon seeing me, Matthew's response was: "I'd still be with you if you always looked like this." (Do boys realize the sweetness behind a statement like that? Are they aware of the magnitude that those words can carry?)

I've been in a relationship where the words, "I just want you to know" were overused and my response, "I'm not a mind-reader," was exhausted. And that relationship...it (obviously) ended.

But, don't kid yourself, Matthew's sweet words were preceded by months of me literally having to say to him, "I Need You To Help Me" when I would have my own questions and doubts about whatever. But boys will learn.

I encourage anyone reading this—guys and girls, daughters and sons—share how you feel when you mean it. You never know when you won't have that chance again.

And if you want a miracle, maybe you have to start by *being* a miracle.

Open Up

It wasn't until I started writing my book that I realized something—Matthew loved me all along. I didn't see the signs until I put them to paper. I simply wasn't aware.

Maybe that's something we should all try to do more often: document our stories. We all have them. When you write your experiences down, you can truly see what's been going on in front of you all along. You finally can open up.

All this time I thought that I was loving Matthew, but it turns out he was loving me. He was always coming to me. Always waiting for me. Always pursuing me. Always being patient with me. Always respecting me. He's been here the entire time, and he didn't give up.

For that, I love him.

Acknowledgements

In the process of writing this book, it became evident how truly blessed I am. As I wrote these short stories of my incredible friends and family, I realized how much I cherish them. I hope I've made you proud. This book is a testament to how truly wonderful each and every one of you are to me.

While in college, I learned about something called the "ah-ha moment." As self-actualizing human beings, we've all likely experienced at least one of these. It's the moment when you realize something significant and are forever changed. It causes you to stop in your tracks and gasp for air. Sometimes, it can even change who you are. This book was my ah-ha moment. It has changed who I am and made my heart more tender and thankful.

If you fell in love with my Matthew, whose real name is Michael, then you know why I have chosen to write about him. Michael, you have helped me to love again, and for that, I am forever thankful.

About the Author

Christie Schroeder is a professional psychotherapist at a group practice in Atlanta, Georgia. She specializes in counseling families, adults, couples, and children, with a primary focus on seriously emotionally disturbed (SED) children in poverty. She has a Master of Arts degree in Professional Counseling, as well as a Bachelor of Science degree in Human Development and Family Studies, and Psychology. She is a member of the American Counseling Association and has formerly worked as a special education teacher. In her debut book, *How to Really Win or Lose a Guy in Ten Days*, Christie draws on her professional background and real-life experiences to entertain and educate her readers.

Made in the USA
San Bernardino, CA
24 December 2013